PRAISE FOR
THE *Voices of the 21st Century* BOOKS

Voices of the 21st Century by Gail Watson is a book that tells the most intimate and traumatic experiences of forty brave women that decided to share it to connect to others and give them hope and understanding while they pass their own problems. This book is part of the Women Speakers Association which has the goal to provide a platform for women to get seen and share their stories to collaborate together to make a difference in the world. The women "speaking" in these chapters are brave women that decided to change their lives and now share their suffering, experience, and results so others can do the same and live a fulfilling and happy life.

—*Quirru, Vine Voice*

Voices of the 21st Century by Gail Watson is a collaborative effort from forty different women who share their personal journeys in this thing called life. By sharing some of their innermost thoughts and secrets and their personal lessons, these women have opened up, allowing us a peek into their psyches. These women share their various challenges and how they overcame adversity. You will love this inspirational collection, the way the women encourage and motivate young women to pursue innovative careers, including those often dominated by men. Overall, this is an engaging read and one that will certainly motivate, make you think, and open up opportunity for women from all walks of life.

—*V.E., Vine Voice*

Times have changed, but the need to help make an impact in the world hasn't, so thank you to all the women who wrote their stories and shared their experiences so more of us can help others, too. It truly feels like a ripple effect.

—*Terra Booe*

In this time of great stress, anxiety, and depression when it seems like there is just one catastrophe and tragic event after another, we could all use some inspirational words of encouragement and some heartwarming stories about people who persevered despite insurmountable odds. Fortunately, Gail Watson's book, *Voices of the 21st Century*, does just that. Watson, president and founder of Women Speakers Association (WSA), a global community of women speakers, gathered forty women who were willing to share their personal struggles and offer advice for readers who are going through their own struggles. In each story, the women of *Voices of the 21st Century* offer encouragement and inspiration. With one voice, they seem to say, "You got this."

—*Julie S. Porter*

I'm reading this book at a time when the world is being battered by coronavirus and we live in fear for ourselves, our family and friends, our health, and our economic future. This book has inspired me and given me hope to face the dark days ahead. These brave and inspirational women show us that self-realization, determination, and resilience have managed to get them through all kinds of situations.

By reading these stories about ordinary women, this book has renewed my mojo, motivating and empowering me to face and embrace the inevitable changes that are ensuing and to not be afraid to listen to that inner voice that will guide me along the way.

—*Elizabeth Darwish*

None of these stories are particularly new—living with cancer or diseases that rip away your self-image and self-esteem; enduring racial inequality and facing stereotypes; overcoming personal loss and tragedy. But these stories are about victory, not victims. These are resilient women with the courage to reflect on their experiences who are now driven to help others.

—*Jenty Young*

I couldn't put this book down! If you are looking for inspiration, uplifting, hope, and positivity, this is the book to grab.

—*Felicia Williams*

If you're feeling devoid of inspiration in these trying times, or hopeless with everything that is going on, then you will certainly get a lot out of this collection. There are many stories of tragedy in this book, but in the tragedy, there is triumph, which makes it a great inspiration to anyone hoping to get out of the funk they are in. There is something remarkable about each one of these stories, so I would recommend reading each one carefully and with an open mind. You might find yourself in some of the stories or discover someone to look up to as you work toward improving your own life. The collection is well put together and seems to flow perfectly in regard to content. I'd recommend this book to any woman, but also to any human being looking to find the beauty and strength in humanity.

—*Chelsey McQuitty*

Voices of the 21st Century is a vehicle to inspire you to pursue your passion and make a difference. These women teach us perseverance, the power of kindness, and how to cope with failure and painful learning experiences.

—*Scarlett Jensen*

The strength and perseverance that each of these amazing women displayed have seen them through their personal struggles and challenges will definitely fuel the fire within yourself. This is definitely a book to be kept by your side to be read and reread because you can draw so much courage and inspiration from each of the forty stories. Definitely a treasure not to be missed!

—*Faith Lee*

This book is addressed to every woman around the globe, but in my opinion, it is a must-read for everyone. It is perfect for the moment we are living: women in society are having more and more participation, and they are gaining force to achieve their goals.

—*Ivana S.*

To see the previous books in the *Voices of the 21st Century* series,
Women Who Influence, Inspire, and Make a Difference;
Bold, Brave, and Brilliant Women Who Make a Difference;
and *Powerful, Passionate Women Who Make a Difference,*
visit www.voicesofthe21stcentury.com/buynow.

VOICES OF THE 21ST CENTURY

*Resilient Women Who Rise
and Make a Difference*

GAIL WATSON

PUBLISHING

Published by WSA Publishing
301 E 57th Street, 4th Fl
New York, NY 10022

Manufactured in the United States of America, or in the United Kingdom when distributed elsewhere.

Watson, Gail
Voices of the 21st Century: Resilient Women Who Rise and Make a Difference
LCCN: 2020923743
ISBN: 978-1-951943-40-0
eBook: 978-1-951943-41-7

Cover design: Natasha Clawson
Copyediting: Claudia Volkman
Proofreading: Deb Coman
Interior design: Claudia Volkman

www.womenspeakersassociation.com

Dedicated to resilient women everywhere, the following poem by Zaneta Varnado Johns captures the essence of this book.

WHAT MATTERS

If your eyes met my eyes in the midst of a crisis,
Would their shape and color concern you?

If you felt my hands as they massaged your aching body,
Would you care about the pigmentation of my skin?

If I gave blood to replenish your low supply,
Would you need to know that I looked like you?

If you were drowning and I dove in to assist you,
Would you reach toward me if you knew I was gay?

If you were hearing for the first time in your life,
Would you need for my voice to speak English only?

If your loved one lay sick and dying,
Would it matter to which god I prayed?

If I donated money to support your favorite cause,
Would you refuse it if you knew how I voted?

If the size of my heart increased each time I helped somebody,
Would you be more interested in the size of my body?

If you asked me to walk a mile in support of humanity,
Would you get impatient if I used my wheelchair?

If I said "no" and you assaulted me anyway,
Are you less guilty because I waited to report?

If my family seeks asylum in the USA,
Are we not welcome because our border is to your south?

If the police force keeps killing unarmed citizens,
Would you demand justice if they are African American?

With civil unrest during this global pandemic,
Trust me, we will soon realize what matters!

CONTENTS

FOREWORD

Gail Watson

Our vision is of a world in which women
Are empowered to authentically express themselves;
To build a thriving, prosperous business;
A world in which women take ownership of
And step into being the leaders that they are;
Using their voice to powerfully inspire others,
Thus causing transformation in the lives of their clients,
their companies, their communities, and the world.
WOMEN SPEAKERS ASSOCIATION'S VISION STATEMENT

Since 2011, I have spoken to thousands of women from around the world, reaching into 120 countries. Each conversation has inspired, moved, and humbled me. I've learned so much and have been honored to hear their stories and how they've served—women of different cultures, countries, ethnicities, religions, and backgrounds speaking their truth, person to person, in a conversation. A common thread is woven through all their tales: a desire to share their voice and unite with others to accelerate their impact to make a bigger difference. As Helen Keller once said, "Alone we can do so little; together we can do so much."

In 2020 we were thrown into a global pandemic and the world as we know it changed, and so did all of our lives. Our countries locked down, our cities shut down, our businesses closed, and our language changed. We had to say no to seeing our friends, no to seeing family, no to leaving our homes . . . the entire world was called to isolate themselves and socially distance. Our hearts broke for what was, and we were left with "now what?"

Because no one is immune—this virus could affect anyone—this pandemic has made us all realize that we are all equal. For the first time ever, it wasn't about a person's status, race, religion, or where they lived . . . we were all vulnerable.

This time may have unmasked and revealed many parts of yourself, making you question yourself and bringing you closer to what you wanted to keep and what you wanted to let go of. Perhaps you experienced feeling happy and sad, angry and grateful, or brave and afraid all at the same time. We became vulnerable while at the same time being courageous—all while grieving for the life that just was. The life we were in control of, the one we could plan and decide the direction we were going, the one where we could simply plan a social gathering with friends. This new reality has forced us to think, question, and challenge ourselves for what is next. Will I reinvent myself? How would I like to reemerge in our new normal? What ideas, beliefs, or actions are now simply unacceptable? How can I make this world a better place?

Women everywhere have stepped up and taken on more tasks within their family units. They carry the emotional stressors of their children, they shoulder the financial pains of their household, they have become schoolteachers at their dining room tables, they are protectors to elderly family members, and so much more. These women are doing it all because they are driven and committed to making a difference in the lives of others.

From the many conversations I've had during this time, I've selected forty women to share their personal messages with you. Theirs are the voices of the everyday woman. These messages will inspire you and guide you. Some may challenge the status quo, while others will bring light to once-dark topics. The common thread running through them all is making a difference and most importantly, letting you know that you are not alone.

These women have come together, representing women from all over the globe. They are spreading their wings to rise and to embrace you. They are here for change. I invite you to read each woman's story with an open heart. Allow her words to fill you. It takes a great deal of courage to share, to be vulnerable, and to speak out, but together we can do it. At this defining moment in history, it is my belief that courageous women will guide us to create and establish a world filled with more love, more acceptance, more equality, and more peace.

Women of resilience are capable of amazing things. During this turbulent year, I've seen how quickly they have opened their hearts, taken charge, and birthed new ideas. Setting aside their own pain and grief, they have expanded their consciousness and set out on a new mission to serve others. With determination and courage, they are willing to stand up for the unacceptable and take a stand against the wrong.

We women are a powerful force!

Gail Watson *is president and founder of Women Speakers Association (WSA), the go-to place for innovative leaders, change-agents, and women with a message to connect, collaborate, and grow their visibility worldwide in order to fulfill their mission. As the first-ever global community for women speakers, WSA provides a platform for women to get seen, booked, and paid AND be part of a growing network reaching women in 120 countries.*

www.womenspeakersassociation.com

The Fairest of Them All

Petisa Anglin

"Mirror, mirror on the wall, who's the fairest of them all?" In the fairy tale *Snow White*, the Wicked Queen commanded her loyal mirror to answer this question. Every day the mirror told her that she was the fairest of them all. And so she was happy. But then one day the mirror told her someone else was more beautiful. Envy and self-hatred consumed her, and she set out on a mission to kill Snow White.

How many times have we looked in the mirror and cringed, shrieked, or just cried because we didn't like what we saw? It might be pimples on our faces, belly fat, saggy skin, droopy boobs, or some other self-claimed flaw we've allowed to diminish our self-esteem. I've heard statements from women like:

"I'm ugly."

"I hate myself."

"I'm not attractive because I don't have large breasts."

"I'd be prettier if my hair was straight or curly or longer."

"If only I was younger . . ."

"I wish I looked like . . ."

Every time I hear these statements, it saddens me that we are not content with ourselves just the way we are.

The Wicked Queen was guilty of believing the lie of the mirror. Why let a mirror define our beauty? It only shows the external components that make up a fraction of our true selves. We're in charge of what we tell ourselves about ourselves. Had the Queen looked further, she could have avoided much turmoil by telling that mirror it was wrong. Unfortunately, like so many of us, she hadn't taken responsibility for her own self-worth or self-love, which is what we as women have to do.

One way to take back our power is through mirror work. Louise Hay used mirror work to help women all over the world learn to love themselves. I've tweaked my own version of it here for you. You'll need a journal to write down your answers.

First, stand in front of a mirror. (If you want a bigger challenge, do this naked.) Now, say the first thing that comes to you about your looks. Don't filter it. If it was a positive statement, congratulations—you know your truth! However, if it was negative, look closer. Remember, only you have the power to decide how you see yourself. Look even closer and pick out the things you would like to change.

Once you're finished, spend about twenty minutes journaling about your experience. Delve deeper into why you want to change those things. Will the change make you happier? Perhaps for a short time. But what you want is everlasting love every time you look in that mirror. If you start right now, right where you are, flaws and all, telling yourself that you love yourself no matter how much weight you need to lose or gain, or how many dimples you have on your thighs, or how knobby your knees are, then you have a greater chance of seeing your true beauty. God created every one of us and He loves us unconditionally, even when we don't love ourselves. Beauty is about who we are on the inside. And we have the power to use that beauty to shine a light for every woman in our lives.

In the second part of this exercise, I want you to take responsibility for your beauty and your happiness by returning to the mirror and intentionally talking to every part of your face and/or body. Be kind and gentle to yourself. It's fine if you don't even believe what you're saying right now. Just say it. Look yourself in the eyes and say, "(Insert your name), I love you." Now take out your list, and while you look at your love handles and your bony ankles, let them know that you love them too. Make it a practice from now on that every time you pass a mirror, you pay yourself a compliment. Give yourself a wink and say, "That lady right there is beautiful." Say it again and again until you believe it. When you're in the shower or as you dress yourself, thank your body parts for bringing you this far and send them love always.

No one could have predicted the strange thing that happened to us on our way to 2021. The world was put on a time-out. Beauty salons, barber shops, and beauty supply stores were all closed for months. We started seeing celebrities, pastors, and news teams as regular people. Hair, beards, and mustaches went unshaven and unstyled. Eyebrows and fingernails went undone. Floppy and missing eyelashes almost became normal. And after all of that, we now must wear masks that cover up the injected lips and tweaked noses we thought made us look beautiful in the first place. Worries over those physical things became unimportant. As soon as the establishments reopened, people hurried off to get the services they were used to. But for a moment in time, beauty was not the focus. Love was.

If you are reading this book, then you made it through the turbulence of 2020, which was a year to pause and reflect. It was a time when the whole world had to look in the mirror and see its true beauty. Don't waste any more time focusing on who is the fairest of them all. Just get out there and love yourself and embrace your beauty. Don't wait for a prince to kiss you to enjoy your life. Go ahead and try new adventures, make new friends, or just have a good belly laugh. Do things that scare you—even if you fail. So what? Once you accept yourself for who you are, you can help another woman on her way to self-love and self-acceptance. Wake up and kiss yourself, Princess, for *you* are the fairest of them all.

Petisa Anglin is an author and writer who enjoys encouraging women. As a Christian and a cancer survivor, she understands the preciousness of life. Volunteering is an important part of her life. She presently lives in South Jersey, where she enjoys spending time with her grandchildren, Penelope and Peyton.

www.iamaphenomenalwoman.com

A MESSAGE OF HOPE

Dr. Lisa M. Bennett

This is a message of hope for women who may be suffering from domestic violence. It is an impassioned cry to love yourself and a reassurance that your faithful actions to secure a better life will be rewarded. You are not alone. You are not unsupported. It is not your fault.

Domestic violence is an international problem. As of 2020, more than one in four women in the United States will have experienced abuse in their lifetime. Men suffer abuse, too, but 90 percent of domestic violence victims are women. The vast majority of the population is unaware that domestic violence is so prevalent. The number of new cases remains the same.

The years since I left my own abusive marriage have been a whirlwind of wonderful travel, loving fellowship with friends and associates from all over the world, gratifying mentoring, and exciting memberships in professional and civic associations. I have been blessed with an intriguing profession that I still enjoy today. But honestly, I did not think about domestic violence after divorcing around 1990.

One evening in 2016, I attended a film called *Finding Jenn's Voice* as part of a domestic violence awareness program offered by the Richmond, Virginia, chapter of the National Coalition of One Hundred Black Women. It was about a woman who was killed by her abusive boyfriend in 2011. It was followed by a panel of survivors and professionals offering inspiration and services to victims.

I experienced a range of emotions that evening. I could hardly breathe as the movie detailed the classic behaviors of abuse. I was dumbstruck as panelists told of their emotional journey through stereotypical abusive relationships. While there has been some progress in legislation for and services available to victims of domestic abuse, I was appalled by the scant amount of media coverage concerning domestic violence. I was disturbed that some still blame the victim. But overall, I was heartbroken that a large number of women still continue to suffer domestic violence decades after my own experience.

My story is typical: attention, loving gestures, and kind words that turned into classic patterns of controlling behaviors and quickly became verbally, emotionally, physically, and even financially abusive. I was fresh out of high school and so inexperienced in life when I met my ex. He had been in the military and traveled a bit. He showered me with attention, and soon it felt natural for him to be around. We married while I was still an undergraduate in college. When I graduated, all he said was, "It doesn't matter how many degrees you get; I will still earn more money than you."

While we were married, my ex terrorized me with alternate episodes of physical violence, verbal and emotional abuse, and threats of economic hardship if I left him. He painted a bleak picture of destitution and loneliness without him. But I wondered how anything could be worse than this. Like 94 percent of abusers, he tried to get me fired from my job by causing scenes at my place of employment. When I tried to leave, things got worse. He threatened to destroy my property, and he also threatened suicide. So I stayed in my marriage against my better judgment. We went back and forth between abuse followed by apologies and good times. I walked on eggshells, not knowing what would set off another verbal or physical attack. My hair fell out from stress. He started dating outside of the marriage. He demanded that I hand over my paycheck to him; I refused. He was a perfect gentleman to family and friends. No one believed me when I told them about his behavior. I decided to leave one night after another verbal lashing. When he went out, I enlisted the help of a few friends so I could move to safety.

I experienced a lot of dissonance—this is very common among victims of domestic abuse. I am here to say: Listen to the dissonance. It is the mismatch between what you are experiencing and what you know to be true. It is a mismatch between the light in your heart and the ugliness from your partner. The truth is that you deserve love, and love does not hurt. Let this light your path and courageously follow it.

Even after I left, my light was but an ember for a long time. I couldn't go back, yet I was scared to go forward. Eventually I thought of returning to college for training as a doctor, and my path was made clear when I was supported by people already in the field. I dreamed of being financially independent and helping others. At the time, this seemed outrageous. I had to go back part-time as an undergrad and work twelve-hour days to achieve my goals. I was ten years older than my classmates. It was expensive.

Your path probably will not be easy either. But, like me, you will be helped and inspired along the way. For every step you take, someone else is taking a step toward you—that's two steps to a brighter future.

Many people helped me, especially my co-workers. I was inspired and emboldened by Tina Turner's book, *I, Tina*. She tells how she only had thirty-six cents when she left her husband, and she only wanted her name so she could rebuild her life. I also wanted my name. Like Ms. Turner, I had to give up the marital assets I had earned in order to get the divorce papers signed. My ex threatened to kill me otherwise. Like Ms. Turner, I was confident in my abilities. I knew I was disciplined and intelligent enough to build a good life. And I have done just that.

My hope is that more people will recognize the signs of abuse. If you are a victim of abuse, I hope you will be confident in who you are and connect with your unique light. I hope you will be inspired to leave immediately. You are not alone. Have faith and love yourself. There really is an abundant life waiting for you if you are willing to go for it.

Dr. Lisa M. Bennett is a graduate of the State University of New York College of Optometry. She is a primary care provider, treating eye disease and performing vision correction. She is a contributing writer for various publications and is currently writing a book about eyes for children.

www.clearviewoptique.com

You Are More Than What People Say or Think

Yasmin S. Brown

"Sticks and stones may break my bones, but words will never hurt me." A childhood saying, one I heard from my family all the time. What if those words came from the one family member you looked up to as a child? My role model was never a celebrity; it was a slender, longhaired, successful African American woman. She was strong, courageous, and a go-getter. This woman was my aunt.

Growing up, I was seen by many adults as "fast" or "hot in the pants," meaning I was growing up before my time. What they did not see was that I was a broken young lady like so many in this world. I hated myself, for lack of better words. I was a girl with low self-esteem, but I wore a mask well to hide the pain I felt inside. Keeping silent rang through my body like nails on a chalkboard. Unfortunately, those nails were internal, not grabbing anyone's attention. Being molested and being in a domestic violence relationship at age thirteen created a physical immunity in my mind. No matter what happened to me physically, I could take it—that is what I always told myself. It was my version of "No weapon that is formed against thee shall prosper" (Isaiah 54:17, KJV). I may not have remembered the actual Bible verse from Sunday school, but I carried the concept.

Even though I put up a mental wall, the bricks were built out of shame, self-destruction, and lack of self-worth. They enabled me to be physically constructed for the world, but not emotionally set up. I was so disciplined in this mindset that I was able to join a drill team as a young girl and focus with a fake smile. The drill team leader was my aunt; she was the person who removed the first brick from my psychological wall, but not in a positive way.

In the beginning we had the best relationship. Pajama parties, traveling, and shopping—every young girl's dream. Then I made a decision that changed the dynamic of our relationship. I was pregnant! By age fifteen, I became a teenage mother. I could no longer be on the drill team, so I had to break the news to my aunt. I watched her pull up in her red compact four-door sedan. I got in the passenger seat and did not waste any time. I blurted out, "I am pregnant!" A few seconds of silence filled the air, and then the most unexpected words pierced my barrier: "You are not going to amount to anything." My heart broke, and I exited the car with no rebuttal.

"He that is without sin among you, let him first cast a stone at her" (John 8:7, KJV) is one of my favorite Bible verses. Negative thoughts are not welcome in a positive environment. Even if my aunt thought such harsh words, they should have remained unspoken. I carried those words in everything I did from that day on—from taking my daughter with me to school every day and making the high school honor roll to graduating college twice. The highlight of those hurtful words was watching my daughter walk across the stage in her cap and gown with her honors cords eighteen years later.

We all carry a burden of words that can either defeat us or propel us into the next endeavors of our lives. I ran into this family member twenty-seven years later, and I was able to forgive her while establishing a boundary that allows me to love her from a distance. Facing and letting go of the heavy weight that followed me for so long was one thing less for me to carry.

Over the years, more bricks started to fall. I released all the emotions I suppressed over time through a self-taught method of "face it, speak it, and heal from it" and therapy. I became more aware of how my past emotionally affected some of the choices I made in my life. This helped me to realize that the words of my past were anchors in my life that I was no longer willing to carry into my future. I declared that 2020 would be a year when I am no longer the doormat, hand towel, or placeholder for anyone's life. I am a pillar in my life. I will stand tall in forgiveness, love, and peace, declaring that I will move forward with God's mercy and grace—with positivity, not only for myself but for others. I will let go of past negativity even if it comes from family. I will not pick up and hold on to new negative environments.

I have learned that by facing whatever holds me back from being my authentic self will no longer have a stronghold on me if I address the issue. The plague of one's past does not need to invade the space of one's today. Forgiveness is the most important part of healing. Learning to forgive was not for my family member; it was for me to be able to move on. I needed to let go and release the control of needing to prove my family member's words wrong.

Reading self-help books to understand my past and walk into my future created a declaration of victory, peace of mind, and strength when facing adversity. I now know that whatever I have been through does not define who I am inside and out. I didn't know what was on the other side of the unknown, but I trusted God, and this allowed me to learn from my experience.

Yasmin S. Brown is an author, empowerment coach, and founder of Yiry-Elements. She is an enthusiastic, self-motivated woman with a paralegal degree in addition to her college diploma in Medical Office Administration. Yasmin's organization helps women with self-expression and personal growth, with a strong focus on mental health.

www.facebook.com/yiryelements

POSTER CHILD OF FAILURE

Carolyn Byrd

You don't drown by falling in the water; you drown by staying there.
EDWIN LOUIS COLE

I am on a call with my content creator; she's digging for my story, wants to understand my journey . . .

I reflect on fun birthdays, times when I celebrated achievements and successes in school, vacations to the lake, the beach, Disney World, snorkeling every summer in the Florida Keys and Hawaii, trips to my grandparents' house, sailing aboard my dad's boat, and time spent with my various horses and traveling around to shows. I share some silly stories of my quirky sense of humor and stubbornness.

These are punctuated and weighed down by more somber memories.

When I was three years old, my dad moved several states away, leaving me with my mom and plenty of emotional baggage. A near-fatal car accident at age seven left me with a big scar across my tummy and a traumatic brain injury. This caused me to be a bit too smart yet a bit too slow, placing me in both advanced classes and curriculum assistance. My mother's remarriage brought new siblings when I was ten, leaving me feeling on the outside of my two families, both of whom were moving forward without me.

By the time I was fifteen, I was forty pounds heavier than most of my friends. I developed an eating disorder that I would cling to until I was twenty-six. Then, cold turkey, I moved across the country to live with my dad and attempt to sort our relationship, which was its own roller coaster of conflicting emotions. I played on white sand beaches, but I self-medicated to numb the pain and silence the tiny voice that said I wasn't enough, wasn't worthy, wasn't wanted.

The years that followed weren't much kinder; a rape in college led me to "inexplicably" drop out with my secrets intact. A failed engagement, severe

GI issues, and a move back to my hometown all left me feeling small and only amplified that not-so-tiny voice.

Life turned around for a while; I graduated college and went on to get my master's degree. I did a ton of yoga and dove deep into triathlons—which I was really good at! I went to therapy and sat with myself (for years); I unwound the traumas and healed my eating issues. I bought a sweet condo downtown and built a massage and coaching business that I am still proud of today. At age thirty I decided to check off a bucket list item and joined the Army National Guard. I went off to basic training with high scores across every entrance exam. Life was good.

And then the bottom fell out all over again. My body failed after taking prescription antibiotics. I was ultimately seen not fit for duty. I felt I had nothing—no home (my condo was rented out), no job (I couldn't be on my feet), little finances . . . my body, mind, and spirit were shattered. There I was, back on a couch at the therapist's office; my fiancé had to carry me upstairs where eight months before I had raced him and beat him to the top.

Back on the call with my content creator, the line is quiet. Then out of her mouth: "My God, you are the Poster Child of Failure!"

And I just laugh. Perhaps she's right.

As I write this, it is my thirty-sixth birthday. I'm reflecting on a recent interview question: "What would the seasoned you tell the younger you?"

My answer: "Not much. Most of my failures and struggles have made me what I am and have taught me so much. I wouldn't want to rob myself of that. I would love to tell the younger me that there is nothing wrong with her. I would encourage her to trust herself and tell her that just because she doesn't fit into 'the boxes' or walk the 'normal' path doesn't mean she's less than or wrong. She's a hell of a lot smarter and capable than she realizes. And, my goodness, she's hilarious!"

There is a heaviness in the word *failure*. It hits you in the gut like a thousand-pound weight. It drags you down into a dark pit and tells you that you are nothing.

But why? Do we not fail and fall a thousand times and more while learning to walk? When do we learn that failure is a mark against our innate value and ability as a person?

By focusing on and dichotomizing failure and success, we miss the gray areas of learning, experience, and growth. If the conversation stops there, we never rise above to fulfill our potential and create our world and the best version of ourselves. We stay in the stagnant place of attaching ourselves to external grading scales that attempt to dictate how we live and define our self-worth. We miss the innate beauty, unique perspectives, and value we each offer as we navigate through this journey of life.

The secret is that there is no score card. There is no standard. You set the standard. You create the goal. Everything else is learning, experience, and growth. Look around. Everything you see around you was created, born from a place of imagination and genius that had yet to exist previously. Before these ideas and things came to be, the mold had to break; it had to fail.

For you to succeed in being the person you dream to be, the person you were born to be, you must fail. You must fail at being what anyone else wanted you to be. You must fail at what you thought you needed to be. You must fail over and over. From this you will learn, experience, and grow into the peace and resilience you must cultivate to succeed.

So, how did you fail today?

Carolyn Byrd is a habit and health coach, massage therapist for both humans and horses, registered yoga teacher, and personal trainer. She has collaborated with many of the top coaches, trainers, therapists, physicians, chiropractors, and mental health-care practitioners. She works with clients of all ages, abilities, and states of health.

www.caryintegrativehealth.com/carolyn-home

MY BLACK IS BEAUTIFUL

Jeannine Rivers Colburn

The year 1963 was a year that made history. Valentina Tereshkova was the first woman to make a solo mission to space. Billboard's Top 100 included two of the most popular songs ever written, "Ring of Fire" by Johnny Cash and "Surfing USA" by The Beach Boys. Zip codes were created, and the world would mourn the death of President John F. Kennedy.

At the same time the racial injustices of 1963 brought about civil unrest throughout the South that would affect the world for many years to come. Protests brought attention to the racial issues plaguing the South, which often resulted in police brutality. The civil rights movement was a determined group of Black organizers fighting to end racial segregation and attain laws that would give Black people the same equal rights as a white person.

This was Southern segregation in 1963: White-only water fountains, bathrooms, department store lunch counters, restaurants, hotels, colleges, public schools, and transportation. But sit-ins (occupying department-store lunch counters and demanding to be served) played a big role in the civil rights movement and set the platform for future changes.

In August 1963, the March on Washington drew attention to the continuing challenges and inequalities faced by Black people a century after emancipation. Over 250,000 people gathered for a peaceful protest. Standing in front of the Lincoln Memorial, Dr. Martin Luther King Jr. delivered his historic "I Have a Dream" speech, offering the Black community hope, inspiring them to dream of a future of peace and equality, and leaving an imprint in the hearts and minds of everyone attending and listening over TV and radio.

In 1963 my dad was thirty years old. He witnessed firsthand the challenges Black people faced in the 1960s. He also remembers being mesmerized as he watched Dr. King's speech on TV. He took that dream and made it his own, adding his own vision and making it a reality for himself and his family.

My birth in October of 1963, during civil unrest and into a society that would judge me based on the color of my skin, gave Dr. King's speech a whole new meaning to my father and also enhanced his own dream. He especially held on to the following words:

> I say to you today, my friends, that in spite of the difficulties and frustrations of the moment, I still have a dream. It is a dream deeply rooted in the American dream. I have a dream that one day this nation will rise up and live out the true meaning of its creed: "We hold these truths to be self-evident, *that all men are created equal.*" . . . I have a dream that my four children will one day live in a nation where they will not be judged by the color of their skin but by the content of their character.

Let Freedom Ring

Growing up, I was never taught that the color of my skin was different or that my skin color would hinder my future. We never talked about racial injustice or my dad's experiences growing up as a Black man. I was taught that I could and would have any and everything in life that I wanted if I worked hard at it. My father set the example by defying the odds and never allowing the color of his skin to dictate what he could do in his life financially and materially.

My father chose to live in a predominantly white neighborhood during a time when it was hard for a Black family to buy a house there. We did not attend a historically Black church. Our place of worship had very few Black people, and the public schools I attended consisted of mostly white people. In fact, all my close friends were white. One day I realized that my whole social community consisted of mostly white people. This did not make me feel uncomfortable because I honestly believed what I was taught: the color of my skin did not make a difference. I was silly enough to think that my outgoing personality, being raised in a upper middle-class Black family, my father's will to live out his dream, and my ability to fit into a white world afforded me the same opportunities of most whites. I learned that this was untrue.

This unusual year 2020 has given me a glimpse of my past and shown me a taste of my unsettling future. I am now faced with the reality of my skin color. At fifty-six years old, I can see and feel the turmoil of 1963. It's as if I have been born all over again. Civil unrest and social injustice is once again plaguing not just the South but the whole world.

Yes, musicians like Lady Gaga are introducing a new kind of music, and legendary musicians like Bob Dylan and Gladys Knight are still making music. But we are dealing with the COVID-19 pandemic, and worldwide, Black people are protesting once again, demanding equal justice, and fighting against racism. I feel a sense of pain that I have never felt in my entire life—pain from my own recent encounters of racism from individuals I have known for most of my life. I feel the aura of hate spreading throughout the land like a cancer. I now know what it feels like to be Black in this America.

My dad, now eighty-seven years old, is disappointed that Black people must still fight for equality. He told me not to lose sight of Dr. King's dream, to make it my own by fulfilling the dream. I now understand that my skin color is different: My black is beautiful.

I will continue to carry out my father's legacy by remembering that "My Life Matters, Black Lives Matter, and All Lives Can't Matter until the World Understands That BLACK LIVES MATTER."

I leave you with this question: What will you do to help end racism in America?

Jeannine Rivers Colburn is the founder and CEO of Illuminate Your Dreams, LLC, a platform where women are educated, empowered, and emerge as confident leaders. Jeannine is the visionary behind Illuminated Women, a group that cultivates women's confidence, empowers them to achieve good mental health, and illuminates the way forward.

www.jeanninerivers.com

DEFY

Michelle Davidson

On September 6, 1980, at the age of four, I boarded a plane with my young mother to leave behind the only home we'd ever known. It was after the devastating 1980 Liberian coup that led to the murder of President William Tolbert. We came to the land of opportunity, and the housing projects in Brooklyn, New York, became our first residence. As undocumented immigrants, we endured dire poverty and drug-infested communities that required us to learn survival rules.

By the age of six, I understood that I should stay alert as I walked home from school and continue to the wrong floor, avoiding using my key to enter our apartment, in the midst of the drug deals happening before me. My mother would call daily and use our code by allowing the phone to ring three times, hang up, and call back again. She left the apartment first thing every morning. She returned close to midnight, working jobs to care for us and send funds for my younger sister still in Liberia. Housekeeping in a prestigious hotel was an opportunity cherished by my mother that came to an abrupt end when it was reported to management that she did not have the proper documentation for employment.

We soon could no longer afford to live in the housing projects and were on the verge of eviction. I took ill around the same time, and I remember my mother asking around for five dollars to buy the medication and supplies I needed to recover. We rested on a mattress retrieved from the sidewalk, and I learned to use my imagination amid no heat and electricity by going camping in our apartment or having candlelit dinners eating pancakes.

If my beginning was a foreshadow of what my life was to become, I would be a by-product of demoralizing circumstances that imprisoned my future. As my mother prayed during the storms of life, she reminded me daily to work hard and excel in school, maximizing every opportunity that came my way and redirecting the course of my life. "'For I know the plans I have for you,' declares the Lord, plans to prosper you and not to harm you, plans to give you hope and a future" (Jeremiah 29:11).

Using television to escape my reality, I began to see through the images portraying the various family dynamics, successes, and opportunities awaiting me. Although my physical environment remained the same, my mind began to shift, awakening me to a new world of possibilities. I was no longer constrained by my environment, and I began to speak to my future and embrace the life before me.

Doubt and opposition are part of the journey, requiring resolve, perseverance, and tenacity to overcome the mountains and valleys of life. I was inadequate in my own strength and found myself fighting what I perceived to be a losing battle. As my intimacy grew with my Savior and Redeemer, I gained the revelation of who I was through Christ that daily strengthens me. No longer did I have to rely solely on my ability to win in life. Instead, I embraced the authority and protection I have through Jesus, renewing my mind and building my confidence to soar in the midst of any circumstance.

As a child, I was displaced regularly due to the socioeconomic challenges that plagued my family. By the time I was twenty-seven, I had positioned myself to open up a mortgage company specializing in the financial strategy necessary to support immigrant families, first-time homebuyers, and those of lower-income in securing their own homes. This platform allowed me the opportunity to share my story at local schools and organizations, fostering hope and possibilities for the future.

In the midst of success, I experienced challenges with my health and was told by multiple doctors I might never have children. In the midst of my despair after receiving this news, I recalled God's promise to me in Jeremiah 29:11. Holding on to the Word of God, I dreamt about marriage and one day having children. Those around me that knew about my diagnosis were concerned about my confession, perceiving I was in a place of denial. Through my journey and experiences, I learned to see the power of faith, word, and action. If I can believe it, speak it, and move on it, I can have it. Three years after my diagnosis, I got married, and I have been blessed to have given birth to three children.

There are greater opportunities awaiting each of us with the prerequisite of pushing past perceived limitations, doubt, fear, and poor self-talk in order to experience the fullness of life. The greatest obstacles facing my life had more to do with my thoughts than the tangible reality of my circumstances. As I confidently spoke to my present and future, breaking free from the limitations of my past and wholeheartedly pursuing the life I desired, I defied the odds stacked against me.

The victories you experience today impact your bloodline, your community, and those you will encounter. By the grace of God, I was able to open up a restaurant for my mom in 2019, where her culinary talents are shared with our local community. A mother that once worked in the factories and took on any odd job she could secure to support her family now has her own business. Our decision to courageously pursue the life we desired has broken strongholds in our lives and in the lives of all those connected to us. My assignment now is helping as many women through the victories and challenges I've developed through winning in all areas of life. I can be a successful professional, wife, mother, mentor, and friend. The circumstances that once stood to discourage and oppress me produced the compassion to lead others effectively. We own our response to opportunity, challenges, and opposition. When we formulate a compelling why for our personal success and faithfully invest in our vision, we defy every obstacle standing in the way of realizing our vision.

Michelle Davidson is a life strategist, personal coach, entrepreneur, and author. She has been a veteran in the residential mortgage industry for over nineteen years. She is the proud wife of Cliff Davidson and mother to Ndiaye and miracle children Jeremiah, Destiny Grace, and Danielle Joy.

www.michelledavidson.life

Claim the Lead

Teena Evert

I'm pedaling before the sun is up. I welcome the fresh, crisp mountain air and the stillness of the early morning. Without much of a warm-up, I begin the 4,000-foot climb up the first mountain pass. My excitement starts to settle as I tune into my increasing heart rate and the steady rhythm of my breath. I know that if I don't pace myself for a long day on my bike, I might not be able to face the challenges ahead and complete the 120-mile ride.

I settle into a gentle cadence as the sun rises over the not-so-distant peaks, and then several thoughts emerge as if to derail me from enjoying the moment. *What if I didn't train enough? What if I'm not strong enough? What if I fail? What if I get hit by a storm?*

Have you ever faced significant challenges in life and doubted your ability to succeed?

How do you keep moving forward when dealing with relentless self-defeating thoughts and extreme external obstacles?

Riding my road bike brings me great joy. Cycling is an endurance sport that requires strength and power. It has taught me a lot about myself and what I am capable of and has significantly improved the quality of my life and the way I handle stress, manage my energy, shift my mindset, and persevere.

For me, growing up was a time of exploration, with no guidance from my parents to keep me safe. I was left to roam and was accustomed to feeling lost and thus not afraid to try new things. My natural curiosity and love of learning gave me enough comfort and guidance to persevere through the hard times.

Self-defeating thoughts developed over time due to how others related to my carefree spirit. I was keenly aware of others and highly sensitive to their fear. I didn't experience care and curiosity from those who inquired about my interests and activities. Instead, I experienced their fear and concern for my ability to think big, take risks, and try new things.

I can remember feeling internally conflicted and thwarted in my ability to express myself fully. I remember a rare occasion of eating out with my family. It was a stressful and uncertain time in our lives, just following my parents' divorce. I was in my senior year of high school and faced with the big decision of what was next. I was excited about the potential path to becoming a surgeon. That desire was squashed in an instant when my family looked at me with shock and disbelief. I never thought about becoming a surgeon again.

My enthusiasm repeatedly got squashed when I was told bluntly, "You don't want to do that" and "You can't do that." These statements did not match how I was feeling, but over time I began to internalize these messages and believe that I didn't know what I truly wanted and that I was not capable of success.

I allowed other people's fear and scarcity mindset to override my state of fearlessness and exuberance for life. As a result, I started to think small, doubt my abilities, and give up too easily when things got hard. I lost my spark of curiosity, and with that came bouts of depression, eroding my self-confidence and creating an anxious mind fixated on all the things that could go wrong. My carefree spirit turned into a heavy heart, and I was stuck fighting with my self-defeating thoughts in a small Midwestern town where small thinking and fear-based living was the norm.

After college, I was able to tap into my desire for freedom and adventure and reignite my zest for life. I moved far away, not realizing I had just started down a long road that would teach me how to live the rest of my life. This road has shown me how to claim the lead in my life and not give my power to fear and self-defeating thoughts and behaviors. It's been a road with many obstacles, points of breakdown, failure, triumphs, and victories.

I'm out for a bike ride; it's midday, 98 degrees Fahrenheit, and the air quality is poor due to multiple wildfires burning across the state of Colorado. I ventured out for a short spin to refocus and reset my mindset after a busy morning with my coaching clients.

I wish I had had a career coach when I was graduating from college. I can remember feeling extremely anxious during this vital life transition because I had no idea what to pursue next. I have changed my career seven times since then. While this demonstrates my fearless ability to take risks, try new things, and navigate significant change, it also shows my lack of guidance, support, and a clear direction.

Facing one's fears, learning to navigate obstacles in one's path, and overcoming adversity are part of everyone's journey. I feel honored to provide the guidance and support that I didn't have throughout my formative years. I didn't have anyone in my life asking me those powerful questions about who I wanted to be and what I wanted to do with my life. Therefore, I love to offer this as a career coach, especially for the younger generation. I love helping them identify their values and create a life and career that aligns with the person they are now and their future self, who they want to become. I help them to be clear about who they are so they can make well-informed decisions, rather than waste a lot of time, energy, money, and resources going down dead-end roads.

I have a passion for speaking and writing about ways to prevent and overcome career burnout, gain confidence during a career change or significant life transition, and cultivate a "claim the lead" mindset. "Claim the lead" is my motto in life. It lights a path of possibility and provides the clarity and confidence to make informed decisions about the future.

Cycling is an endurance sport that requires strength and power, as does creating a life worth living. Having clarity and confidence in yourself is what powers your wheels. It propels you forward into the terrain of self-exploration. You're empowered to take hold of the handlebars and begin to travel down your own unique path of potential that leads to limitless possibilities.

Teena Evert hosts The Confident Careerist *podcast and is the CEO and founder of* CLAIM THE LEAD. *She is a board-certified career coach, certified career transition and hidden job market coach, certified global career development facilitator, certified trauma-informed career counselor, professional resume writer, and licensed mental health professional.*

www.teenaevert.com

Believe It into Being

Rochelle Finzel

I sat in my gown, looked around at the sterile metal cabinets, and clasped my hands tighter. The door opened, and four women in white coats filed into the room, three lining up against the cabinet as the surgeon came over to me, her hand outstretched.

My body tensed and my jaw tightened. My little lumps surely did not require four people to remove; they were the size of peas. Were the four women here to dissect and analyze me like a lab rat? I nervously extended my hand and scanned the doctor's face for any expression that might hint at the seriousness of my procedure.

The churn in my stomach told me it was bad. Flashbacks of the past two years telling people my job was killing me flooded my head as I wondered how true those comments could be. But I didn't work on the weekends. I ran and hiked and even biked to work. My diet was full of fruits and vegetables, and I was always in bed before the news. Surely that counted for something. Not to mention the monumental changes I made in my life to rid it of bad relationships and open myself to new ones.

The internal debate continued over the course of the week following the biopsy. The highs and lows and the pendulum of paralyzing fear to confident optimism played out as I ran a personal-best marathon, nearly reaching my goal of qualifying for the iconic Boston race. Hours after the race, my boyfriend and I drove to Utah for our first vacation together.

Driving through Zion National Park reminded me of a cathedral, the road a narrow nave leading to the altar where the canyon closes in to form The Narrows. I knew I was dying, and I offered my fears and laid my soul to rest in the natural chapel. Death appeared everywhere in the black-stained walls and ravens that flew above.

On the fourth day of our vacation, the doctor called to tell me that the biopsy results indicated that the cancer I had twelve years prior had spread. The lumps were stage-four metastatic melanoma—deadly tumors. Phone in my lap, I stared at the red sandstone boulders in the pullout where we parked imagining myself hairless and gaunt, soon to be gone from this earthly existence. My premonitions were confirmed.

I looked over at my boyfriend and sobbed into his shoulder as I said, "I do not want to die."

As we walked through the fantastical shapes of the hoodoos and rock formations of Bryce Canyon, I saw colors more vividly and shapes more clearly. The orange hue created a glow as if a million candles burned in the canyon. The energy of that fiery light filled in the cracks of doom and darkness that had seemed to permeate my soul just minutes before.

I felt a sense of peace being outside in the natural world with its blue skies and amazing rock formations, the trees jutting out amidst the orange sandstone. The rest of the world disappeared as I savored the beauty and allowed myself to just be in its presence. I found strength and hope in that canyon in the healing arms of Mother Nature.

My old ways flew away like the ravens in the sky. The image of the smart, stoic, and self-sufficient single woman who needed no one shattered. Suddenly I needed everyone. I wanted people to know me—the real me. I did not want to die hidden and afraid.

I opened myself to the world in hopes of soaking in as much of life as possible in the nine months the doctors said I might have left to live. Freed from the illusion of time and tomorrows, I removed the armor that protected me from life's pain and realized the joy that comes from living. From being seen and heard and loved. From seeing and listening and loving in return.

The confidence and clarity from surviving gave me the courage to take on a new leadership role in my organization, and I seized the opportunity to build a team and create a new vision. Feeling invincible, I took chances and dreamed bigger than I thought possible.

I found success in my new position, achieving a level of material wealth that felt like the icing on the cancer cake. I had made it. I not only beat stage-four cancer, but I also landed my dream job and got married, all in the same year.

Two months after our wedding, the cancer came back. I carried needles and drugs on our honeymoon hiking trip and again allowed Mother Nature to heal my spirit. The following fall a suspicious mammogram led to further tests and breast cancer worries. The next PET scan showed a tumor on my ovary. I finally got the hint after my friend died of the same disease I had. I could no longer risk the possibility of dying without trying to truly live.

Quitting my job felt like failure, but I knew in my heart the path to my healing and true purpose in life did not involve business suits and political discussions. Somehow, I had to find a way to be the person that emerged in that canyon in Utah and who always showed up on trails in the middle of the wilderness or the tops of mountains—free and vulnerable. Exposed and raw. Pushed to my limits and proud. Present and reflective. There must be a way to use that person for good.

I discovered the power of coaching and immediately knew it fit my desire to give others the gift that cancer gave me. To help women find their voice, choose their path, and own their power. And now, whether it is finding a job that aligns with their vision and values, starting a new business, or taking on a bigger leadership role, I help others step up and into their purpose with confidence. I believe we are capable of much more than we think if we only have the courage to take the first step and trust that the path will reveal itself.

Rochelle Finzel is a leadership coach, writer, speaker, and outdoor adventurer. She has degrees in leadership and social welfare, having spent twenty years leading public policy and nonprofit efforts to advance economic opportunity. She has a gift for seeing people's strengths and helps high-achieving women thrive in work and life.

www.finzelconsulting.com

CULTIVATE LEADERSHIP

Dr. Juanita Foster

While in college, one of my assignments was to answer the question, "Are leaders born or made?" As I researched the answer, I concluded that the answer is both. Leaders are both born and made. There are numerous articles and research on birth order and leadership. Many of those articles state that being the firstborn means a person is destined to be a leader. Being the firstborn in my family, I completely understand. Growing up, I had to be a leader in many situations, even before I completely understood what being a leader meant. Over the years, I understood that, although I was born in a leadership position, I must cultivate the leader in me. The cultivation of leadership is a process.

In my training classes, I usually ask the class these questions: "Do you know someone who you think is a good leader?" and "Do you know someone who you think is a bad leader?" Then I tell them that I have been both. When I was in a leadership role and completed a project, it was not until after the project was completed that I knew whether my leadership was considered good or poor. Although getting the job done is what leaders do, how they lead is important as well.

There was a time when I was passed up for a leadership position, not because of my skills and knowledge as a leader, but because of the way management and my co-workers saw me. It hurt not getting a job that I felt I was qualified for, but it made me do a self-examination. That was when I understood that cultivating the leader within me was vital. As I started on this journey of self-examination to grow as a leader, I looked at several areas in my life: self-awareness, vision, and resiliency.

Self-Awareness: Being self-aware can be challenging for a leader. In order to be self-aware, one must do self-examinations. I had to do the hard work of letting go of the negative traits that were keeping me from being self-aware: being arrogant, insensitive, and inconsiderate. Doing a self-examination is difficult and rewarding at the same time. It was frightening to confront myself. I decided that I wanted to be free from the old me. To be completely free required that I pray and forgive. I took time to pray to God, asking him to forgive me for dishonoring him.

In my opinion, forgiveness comes in three parts: forgiving yourself, forgiving others, and asking for forgiveness from God and others. Any one of these three parts of forgiveness can be difficult, but when you have to do them all, it can seem impossible. However, it is possible to give and receive forgiveness. In addition to forgiveness, a self-aware person is one who understands who they are and how they react to situations in their life. For example, I learned that when I reacted to situations in haste, my emotions led me to say and do things negatively. As of a result, this led to poor leadership on my part. I had to learn how to manage my emotions. The benefit of managing my emotions, praying, and working on forgiveness is self-awareness. A leader who is self-aware leads with integrity and a clear vision.

Vision: On my journey to grow as a leader, I've come to understand the importance of having a vision. Having a vision can mean different things for different people. My vision had to answer several questions for me. What type of leader did I want to become? How did I want to lead from this point forward? And what kind of legacy did I want to leave? It lit my path to achieve success in many areas of my life. Honestly, throughout the years, my vision has changed. As I answer the questions about my leadership at different points in my life, I course-correct my vision so that I remain on track. The vision that I create for myself is not just for me, but for my family as well. Just as in the business world, my family is my team. Leaders must have a vision for themselves, their organization, and those they lead. As the Bible states, people perish because of the lack of vision.

Resiliency: My definition of *resiliency* is "the ability to bounce back." There have been many failures and setbacks in my life. Being in an abusive relationship, losing a baby, being passed over for a promotion, not getting a particular job—the list goes on and on. However, learning how to be resilient has shaped the way that I live my life and the way that I lead. After not getting the job I previous mentioned, I had to become more resilient. Being resilient takes mindset work. There were countless times when I sat on the side of my bed talking to myself, telling myself, "I can do it." That mindset work enabled me to really see myself in a better place, and in turn,

I was able to lead better. In the business world, there are so many things that can cause a leader to fall and not get back up. When a leader is able to shake off the failures, those setbacks give them the strength to be a more effective leader.

In conclusion, as I continue my life's journey, I am still working on cultivating the leader in me. As I get older, I realize that I have to continually develop myself as a leader. It doesn't matter if you lead others or not. *You are the first person you lead.* I am approaching my fiftieth birthday, and I am still learning how to lead myself. As business owners, it is important for us to continue to develop self-awareness, vision, and resiliency to grow ourselves, our families, and our businesses. So cultivate leadership!

Dr. Juanita Foster is a life coach, international leadership and team development speaker, trainer, and consultant. She is the lead consultant and CEO of Educate Motivate Elevate Consulting, LLC, located in Delaware. For more than twenty years, she has been conducting leadership workshops and seminars for corporations and individuals.

www.drjuanitafoster.com

THIS IS WHO I AM!

Sunny Fridge, PhD

I was once afraid of people saying, "Who does she think she is?"
Now I have the courage to stand and say, "This is who I am."
OPRAH WINFREY

Have you ever been afraid of people saying, "Who does she think she is?" That quote by Oprah Winfrey was an aha moment for me. I had the opportunity to meet Oprah when I was an aspiring young television reporter living in Queens, New York, chasing my dream. I worked as a secretary at the CBS television network. I didn't have a degree at the time, but I had passion. A veteran cameraman named Tony Ancona knew I wanted to be a journalist and took me under his wing.

Thanks to Tony, I had a backstage pass to many events. My favorite was attending the 14th Annual Daytime Emmy Awards, which honored the best in broadcasting. Oprah was nominated for her first "Emmy Award for Best Talk Show Host for Television" and "Best Daytime Talk Show." She was my role model. If she won, I would get to interview her! The competition was stiff. Oprah was up against long-time Emmy winner and talk show host Phil Donahue. What a thrill when Oprah won! It was her first year as host of a national TV show. She told the audience she didn't prepare a speech because she didn't think she would win. She was interviewed by an alphabet soup of media outlets: NBC, ABC, CBS, CNN, ET. And then there was me. I suppose if I had station call letters, they would have been SFQ: Sunny From Queens.

I remember anxiously waiting until Oprah finished her interviews with the major networks. To say I was nervous was an understatement. My heart was racing a mile a minute. I had butterflies in my stomach, and I was afraid I wouldn't be able to speak. More importantly, would Oprah want to speak with me? After all, who did I think I was? My cameraman told me to put my game face on and go for it. Slowly I walked, step-by-step . . . gaining confidence along the way. As I approached her, I said a silent prayer: "Dear Lord, don't let me faint." And then I spoke. "Hi, Miss Winfrey, I know you've been interviewed so many times, but I wanted to ask you, how does it feel to win?" I held my breath as she looked at me. Oprah smiled and said, "That's a question I never get tired of answering." Oprah continued to speak with me as if I, Sunny From Queens, was just as important as all the other media. I was on cloud nine! At that moment, I no longer worried about who people thought I was. It was a defining moment in my life.

Today I am a presentation skills coach and trainer. Did you know when you google "presentation skills coaching," there are over 148 million results? If I didn't believe in myself, that would be enough to make me pack up "my tips, tools, and techniques" and take my seat in the audience. I often share my Oprah story with emerging speakers, entrepreneurs, and rising leaders. I remind them that there may come a time in their life as they pursue their dreams when someone will ask, "Who do you think you are?" Sometimes it may be the voices in their own minds that say, "You don't have the right education or qualifications. What about that time you failed?"

I don't know what you're going through or the obstacles you've faced in achieving your dreams. But I do know that if you want to silence those mind monsters, you've got to grab your fear. You've got to grab your faith and make faith BIGGER than your fear of failure. Studies show that when it comes to "self-talk," your brain doesn't know the difference between a truth and a lie. And what you think and say to yourself impacts your belief of who you are. Henry Ford said, "Whether you think you can or you think you can't, either way you're right." The good news is that we can retrain our brain. We can scare those mind monsters away with positive affirmations. "I am fearfully and wonderfully made." "I am a winner." "I am good enough!"

The Law of the Inner Circle states that you are the sum of the five people closest to you. Get a dream team—people who support you and aren't afraid to help you rise and shine. My cameraman Tony was part of my dream team before I even knew what a dream team was! I later found out that Tony had been a cameraman for legends such as CBS news anchor Edward R. Murrow and TV greats Jackie Gleason and Ed Sullivan. His willingness to mentor me is a big reason why I continue to mentor young people and empower others to become the best versions of themselves.

For fifteen years I served as a journalism educator at a local university. I loved sharing my experience and skills as an award-winning broadcaster and producer to help students become reporters, producers, and storytellers. But in 2015 there were leadership changes, and my contract was not renewed. This was a difficult time in my life. It's been said that a setback is a setup for a comeback! I did what I'd always encouraged my students to do. I began to "dream big." Thanks to Toastmasters and the John Maxwell team, my "comeback" is empowering speakers, entrepreneurs, and rising leaders to communicate and confidently connect with the audience they are called to serve.

As we continue to face unprecedented times of uncertainty, I encourage you to rise above your fears and doubts to dream big. Whether you want to be a world-class speaker, write a book, or start a new business, it's not too late. Learn to trust God and His plans for you. Live your dream with purpose and passion. And step-by-step, you'll gain confidence along the way to walk into your destiny and say, "This is who I am!"

Sunny Fridge, PhD, is an award-winning professional educator and communications consultant. She is a certified coach, speaker, and trainer with the John Maxwell team. She is host of Rise & Shine with Dr. Sunny, *an online show and podcast that empowers emerging speakers, entrepreneurs, and rising leaders to become better communicators.*

www.sunnyfridge.com

Becoming American:
A New Beginning

Gudy Grewal, MA, MSW

It was a beautiful Miami morning. I woke up early, and through the window in my hotel room, I watched the sunrise. It was a new day and a new beginning. The temperature was in the seventies—balmy by the standards of my current home in Denver, Colorado. On that morning, I found myself refreshed by the coolness of the air and the gentle breath of the ocean breeze. As I looked out the window, I was struck by the intensity of my emotions.

It was finally here—the much-awaited day of Tuesday, November 3, 1987. Later that morning, I was to become a citizen of a country for the first time in my life. Not only that, but this was the day I was going to take my oath to become an American citizen, a country I considered to be the greatest in the world.

For me it was especially surreal because I had never been a citizen of any country. Despite having been on the planet for more than three decades, I was a person without a state. I had lived in many different countries, mastered several languages, integrated into different cultures, and faced many atrocities. Yet I did not belong to any nation. I could not call any place my own. Sure, I had a British Protectorate passport, but that was more of a travel document and did not make me a British subject. However, on this cool November day in Miami, all of that was going to change. I was finally going to become a citizen of the United States of America. I was becoming an American.

Though I tried to savor my morning coffee, my mind was on the events ahead. After my last sip, I took out my dress from the wardrobe where I had placed it the day prior. For weeks, I had considered wearing a sari (an Indian female national dress) to the ceremony. But in the end, I decided to buy myself a new dress. I wanted to dress as an American.

It was a simple black cotton dress with a red, white, and blue print. As I looked at my dress in the mirror that morning, I realized that even though I had not planned it, I had picked the colors representing my new nation. I dressed carefully, put on black pumps, and walked down to my car, trying not to reveal my excitement to the other hotel guests. Today, I was going to witness an auditorium full of people from different parts of the world who, like me, were going to finish a long journey toward their destination of becoming American.

As I crossed the threshold into that room, I was given a brochure and an American flag.

To one side of me, there were people who spoke a language that I did not understand. Nonetheless, I felt a sense of comradery with them. Even though none of my family members had come with me, I did not feel alone. After all, thousands and thousands of immigrants like me had taken the same path. In fact, for over two centuries, foreign-born men and women from all over the world had taken some form of an oath of allegiance to become American citizens (the current Oath of Allegiance was formalized sometime in the 1950s).

Promptly at 9:00 a.m., a woman who seemed less excited than the rest of us announced that the honorable judge was going to enter the auditorium. We all stood as the judge quietly entered and sat down. Almost as if the entire scene were choreographed, all of us immigrants sat after the judge sat. First, he welcomed us. Then, somewhat to my surprise, he gave us a very heartfelt and personal speech. He told us that he was of Italian descent. His parents, like many of us, were first-generation immigrants. He reminisced about how his father had served in the U.S. Army during the Second World War, and he told us that he was a veteran of the Vietnam War—as if to remind us that our citizenship came with a great sense of duty. He also talked about how meaningful it was for his parents, naturalized American citizens like me, to have a son who grew up to be a judge in this great nation.

I was touched. I realized as the judge spoke that his parents must have taken the same Oath of Citizenship that I was about to take. As he ended his remarks, the critical announcement was made: "All rise." The whole auditorium—immigrants from all over the globe—stood in unison, and we all raised our right hands. For me, however, the oath was probably a little different. The very first sentence—"I absolutely renounce and abjure all allegiance and fidelity to any . . . state or sovereignty . . ."—began a cascade of tears rolling down my face. I had no other state to renounce.

Today, I was thousands of miles away from where my life's journey had begun in Dares-Salaam, Tanzania. I always joked with people that I had taken the scenic route to reach America.

Today, I belonged to the nation of Presidents Kennedy and Lincoln. So did the hundreds of people who took the oath with me. We did not know each other, but we will always have one thing in common: No matter where we came from, we were all now Americans. Standing in that auditorium, I felt that I was one of luckiest people in the world. I was free, and I had the Constitution of this great country to back me up.

And yet, becoming an American citizen was just the beginning. I had not yet realized the full impact of who I was going to be. I had not internalized what becoming an "American" really meant. On that day, I was simply elated to have a country where I belonged and the United States of America to call my own. It was a new beginning.

Gudy Grewal, MA, MSW, is a clinical social worker and an intercultural-competence consultant. Born in Tanzania and having lived in five countries over four continents, Ms. Grewal is proud to be an American citizen. She provides coaching, offers trainings in intercultural competence, and is an exceptional speaker.

gudygrewal@aol.com

From Misery to Miracles

Cherie Griffith-Dunn

I learned at a young age that life is not fair. Good things were only for certain people and I wasn't one of them. "Why me?" I screamed silently, but there was never any answer. The pain was so unbearable that I wanted to disappear. *Maybe that would make it hurt less*, I thought.

Ever since I was a young girl, I listened, I did all my schoolwork, I was respectful—unlike my sisters. But they all seemed to have amazing lives, and I did not. "Life is so unfair," I told myself.

I asked my mother why I was so miserable and in so much pain. She tugged at her hair and took a deep breath. She stared at me with sadness in her eyes and said, "Baby, it will be okay—I promise."

I didn't know if I could believe her, but there was something different about her voice that day. I reached out to hug her, but before I could, she touched my shoulder and grabbed my hand with a tight squeeze as if to say, "It better be all right."

I will never forget that spring day in 1989. I will never forget that day because it was the worst day of my life. It was the day I received news that would forever change my life. You see, on that sunny spring day, my doctor told me that I would never have children. I had developed a severe case of endometriosis and would need to be on medication for as long as I could bear the pain, and then I would have to have a hysterectomy at a young age. He said it was the only way, that there was nothing else he could do, and he walked out of the examining room with his head down. I went numb and began shivering uncontrollably, not really understanding what he said. I knew it was bad, though, when my mother turned away and put her hands together to pray, asking God, "Why, why? She does not deserve this." On the way home neither of us spoke, and I felt so empty inside.

The day I graduated high school was a day of true reflection—unlike my friends who couldn't wait to go to the after-grad party. I was more interested in thinking about what my adult life would be like. I felt hollow inside, frightened by the butterflies in my stomach and the tears in my eyes. It was as though life had stopped for me, while everyone else's lives were filled with fun, laughter, and love. Oh, how I wished I could someday have that too.

I hid under my covers in my room the following week, wishing that one day I would wake up and be okay. One night as I drifted off to sleep, I heard a tap at my window. It was my girlfriend asking me to come outside and go to some party. I told her no. I was not in the partying mood; I was too busy thinking that life had ended for me.

I found myself distancing from everyone and everything—my family, my friends, and the one thing I loved most: running. When I went for a run, I knew I was alive, but now I had nothing to live for, so there was no need to do something I enjoyed ever again.

We all have the tendency to push ourselves deeper and deeper down when we do not see another way out. We begin blaming everyone and everything. Days and weeks went by as I fell deeper into depression. I refused to bathe, eat, or even get out of bed.

Do you believe that life can change in an instant? I'm here to tell you that I do! I have lived it and watched it happen to me. Fast-forward to 1996. I was now married, and my husband and I decided that we would go against what that doctor told me about being infertile; we would try to have a baby. We found an amazing doctor who specialized in in vitro fertilization, and we figured it was worth a try. The day we were accepted as candidates in the program, tears of joy ran down my face. I could not believe there was a possibility that I could have a child. The weeks leading up to the transfer, I was a nervous wreck. I was bombarded by every negative thought—*This is not going to work. Why are you doing this to yourself? Girl, you are crazy*, and so on.

Our minds are so powerful and dangerous at the same time. I never realized that my thoughts could keep me in a dark place. I guess I always viewed my mind as the operation command center that had all the answers to pull me out of trouble. But now I was learning that my mind only reflects what I tell it. So I decided to pray and think positive thoughts about how amazing it would be to have this precious baby.

The results were finally in! I was pregnant! I was filled with joy. Every day was touch and go, but eight and half months later, I delivered a healthy baby boy. And that's not all—I went on to give birth to five other baby boys! Yes, you heard right—after being told that I would never have children, I now have six amazing sons!

And I went back to running! "For we walk by faith, not by sight" (2 Corinthians 5:7).

If you struggle with a painful diagnosis or life seems unfair and you don't know why, don't give up! Life is full of surprises, and if you replace all those negative thoughts with positive thoughts of faith, you'll be amazed at what can happen. Be resilient, walk by faith, and expect a miracle.

Cherie Griffith-Dunn is a transformation catalyst, leadership and executive trainer, and highly sought-after motivational speaker. She offers programs for rising executives and entrepreneurs to step into their power and grow their careers and businesses. Cherie has helped over one thousand rising leaders go from good to great using her seven E.L.E.V.A.T.E Your Life Principles.

www.cheriegriffithdunn.com

A Series of Moments—
How Will You Spend Yours?

Charmaine Hammond

"Life is a series of moments . . . moments that define you, stretch you, challenge you, and make you grow. The question is, how will you spend your moments?" I penned this quote almost twenty-five years ago after surviving a near-death sailboat accident. That day in the lake, as my then-boyfriend Chris and I found ourselves swimming for our lives, was comprised of a series of moments that shaped who I have become and who I am today. In fact, in many ways that day in the lake is an anchor for me. Not an anchor that keeps me stuck, but an anchor that keeps me grounded and connected to what (and who) matters most.

That day taught me about surrender, about love, and how sometimes moments need to happen to complete the story.

After swimming for several hours, Chris became hypothermic and was drifting in and out of consciousness. When he thought he would not make it back to shore, he told me I needed to leave him and go get help. He believed that I would make it to find help, but he knew his time was limited. What I didn't realize at the time was that Chris was really saying, "I'll swap my life for yours." He also told me, "When we get back to shore, we have a wedding to plan." His words gave me permission (and courage) to leave him to get help.

We were eventually rescued, and one year later, as Chris promised, we were married and will soon be celebrating our twenty-fifth anniversary. I often lovingly tease him saying, "Poor guy, you didn't think you were going to make it. Now you are stuck with me." I am so glad he is stuck with me, because he has been my rock more times than I can count.

Life really is a series of moments. Sometimes at the time, moments don't make sense or may perhaps seem irrelevant. As I took time to reflect during these times of physical distancing in a pandemic and having more time to just "be," it seems that in hindsight, these life moments when strung together were all supposed to happen in order for the next great (or not so great) moment to take place. One thing I know for sure is that without these series of moments, I would not be who I am today, and life would look a lot different. And I really like how life looks right now!

In 2018 a series of moments occurred that quite honestly took the wind out of my sails but later gave me strength, courage, a renewed confidence and trust in myself, and a deep appreciation for the string of moments that had gone by.

I was diagnosed with breast cancer.

Truth be told, walking into my appointment with the radiologist, I think I already knew the answer. I don't know how I knew, but somehow I knew. Later that night, as angry and afraid as I was, I remember thinking that maybe life had prepared me for this. I could get through this. In fact, I needed to get through this! I had survived a fire in the house I rented during my first career after college; I survived dangerous situations when I worked as a correctional officer; and I survived a near-death sailboat accident. I was committed to surviving this crisis as well. I have too much I still want to do while on the planet, so I committed to doing what I needed to get better. Just like the sailboat accident, having cancer and all the moments wrapped up in that taught me about surrender, love, the heroes I have in my life, and how sometimes moments need to happen to complete the story.

Things moved quickly once the diagnosis was confirmed. In less than six weeks I had a mastectomy, and then over the next six months, I had another surgery and more than fifty-four visits to the doctor, health nurses, and clinic, four rounds of chemo, and twenty-eight injections to rebuild my immune system. I had to get used to people helping me, and I had to get comfortable with asking for help (Chris lovingly points out there is still some work for me to do on this goal).

Many people in my life reading this will be very surprised, as they will not have known about me having cancer. I chose to deal with this in a private way so I could focus 100 percent of my energy on regaining my health and nurturing my closest relationships.

I am now a year and a half post-chemo and doing really well. I love my curly hair (it was always bone straight), and my scars have faded and are just really part of who I am now. I hardly even notice them, and when I do they remind me of the love, support, and encouragement that I received from others and that I did it—I'm still here! I don't have any drama attached to cancer, just deep appreciation and love for the people in my life who swapped their moments to help me during mine.

Even though having cancer was one of the scariest and painful experiences I've dealt with, there aren't too many moments that I would want to swap, because each of these moments was like a gift wrapped in sandpaper—and I think that also gave me life!

Be open to the moments that happen in your life, even if they don't make sense at the time or are difficult and painful to experience. Find the champions and your trusted family and friends to experience the moments with you, and remember, it's okay to ask for help. Kindness is not just about how you show up and treat others. Kindness means giving, including giving kindness to ourselves, so treat yourself with kindness!

Embrace these moments of your life because in the end, they will define you, challenge you, stretch you, and help you grow.

*Resilience expert **Charmaine Hammond** is a highly sought-after keynote and workshop speaker, author, and business owner who teaches the importance of developing trust, healthy relationships, and collaboration in the workplace. She has helped corporate clients build resilient, engaged teams, develop high trust/accountability relationships, and solve the tough issues that impact success.*

www.charmainehammond.com

RESILIENCE, RISING UP, AND SHARING MY VOICE

Nadine Hanchar

I always knew that I was adopted. Please do not feel sorry for me! I was absolutely accepted and loved as a daughter, sister, grandchild, niece, and cousin. I used to quite proudly tell people that I was adopted until my mother asked me to stop because she didn't want me to get hurt. Out of respect for her, I stopped telling people unless it was relevant.

What has always amazed me, though, is the perception of adopted children from people who aren't adopted. Since I didn't fit those perceptions and I wasn't telling people I was adopted anymore, people assumed that I was not. Apparently adopted children are supposed to be troublemakers—difficult and delinquent children who always want to find their birth parents. I was none of those things.

I will share with you an awkward incident with a teacher I had in grade eight. As a student, we would write speeches and present them to the class. To give the students an example, the teacher gave the whole class a speech on adopted children and why they had so many problems. Needless to say, I was shocked and upset that a teacher would give such a speech.

My first speech was titled "Why Adopted Children Are Misunderstood." I talked about how people often make adopted children feel bad if they don't want to look up their birth parents. How they encourage them to feel weird about being adopted. How they make assumptions about adopted children not being well-adjusted, capable, and well-behaved individuals.

I explained in my speech that many adopted children are very well-adjusted people who positively contribute to their families. I explained that adopted children are often treated by their families exactly the same as children who have been birthed into the family. I concluded my speech by saying, "If you have any more questions about well-adjusted adopted children, please feel free to ask me about it, since I was adopted into a family of both birthed and adopted children." I ended with the statement, "I do not fit the picture of a delinquent or ill-behaved child, and I am not interested in knowing who my birth parents were because I have parents whom I love and who love me!"

Now, while I was giving my speech, I kept a close eye on the teacher. I was amazed that just like in the cartoons where a flush comes up and down the face of the cartoon character, it can happen in real life too. To give that teacher credit, I did get an "A" on my speech—and an apology.

I did know other adopted children, one girl in particular who used to get out of trouble by playing the "feel sorry for me 'cause I'm adopted" card. She knew I disapproved because I knew she didn't really feel that way!

I've lost count how many times the first question someone asked me when they found out I was adopted was, "Don't you want to find your birth parents?" I found this very insulting and hurtful to me and the parents who raised me. Yet people wanted me to feel that way! The person who gave me up for adoption I'm sure had good reasons for doing so. Why would I want to disrupt their life or mine by going and digging up the past?

My belief is that you come into the world through your birth mother, but the parents that raise you and the family you grow up in are the ones you were meant to be with. They are the ones who ultimately give you the wounding and the blessings that you were born to work through and learn about in this lifetime. This is true for everyone.

My family was far from perfect, and yet so much of what I have learned about life and what truly matters came from them. I became an adult at a young age because of my mother's inability to cope with my brother's death. Because my dad was sought after in his career, we moved a lot, and I struggled with having to start over so many times. It wasn't easy, but I learned, I forgave, I loved, and I worked on my relationship with myself.

Standing up for what you believe in allows you to respect yourself. When you respect yourself, others learn to respect you. Being authentic creates inner strength and confidence. There have been so many times in my life when I have been knocked down, betrayed, or put down and told I couldn't do something. Instead of believing in what others were saying and playing small, I have chosen to learn from those experiences, get up, dust myself off, and move forward.

As an NLP trainer, one of the principles I teach is: "There are no mistakes, only feedback and learning." When you really apply that principle to your life, it can change it completely. I know for myself it has changed how I view life and how I live it.

Many times as a counselor I hear people say to me, "It's easy for you because you have high self-esteem." Yes, I do now, and how I got here was by learning to respect, accept, and develop a good relationship with myself—the good, the bad, and the ugly. I learned how to say no—a wonderful little word. I learned to be authentic with myself first and then with others. I learned to have a voice and use it. I learned from my experiences, even when it was hard. I developed the understanding that respecting others acknowledges their right to make their own mistakes (learnings). I developed my self-esteem by always being willing to get back up again!

My hope is that you, too, will develop an attitude of curiosity, resilience, and respect for yourself!

Nadine Hanchar is the developer of the PEP Personality Process and an NLP master trainer, speaker, facilitator, counsellor, consultant, and bestselling author. Specializing in relationships, trauma, communication, and professional development, her results-oriented approach allows individuals, couples, families, or organizations to go forward with a better quality of life.

www.progressiveplus.com

Invisible No More

Zaneta Varnado Johns

If your eyes met my eyes in the midst of a crisis,
Would their shape and color concern you?
If you felt my hands as they massaged your aching body,
Would you care about the pigmentation of my skin?

If you were hearing for the first time in your life,
Would you need for my voice to speak English only?
If your loved one lay sick and dying,
Would it matter to which god I prayed?

The above is an excerpt from a poem I wrote in June 2000, "What Matters," and then updated in May 2020, after the onset of COVID-19 and the continued unjust police shootings of African Americans. I felt compelled to add thoughts concerning the *Me Too* movement, our country's recent stand on immigration, and its toxic divide based on political party affiliation. The fact that I *added* to this reflective poem tells me that our country is moving in the wrong direction!

I grew up with five siblings in the segregated South, neither privileged by socioeconomic standards nor by America's absurd racial hierarchy. We were privileged, however, to be raised by hardworking parents who taught us by their fine example that everyone had value. I knew my value early on, and I knew what mattered. With love, I've demonstrated that notion by how I live.

I raised two children who also know without question their value and who respect everyone. It was not always easy for them growing up in predominantly white Boulder, Colorado. An African American child whose cultural "village" accounts for 1 percent of a city's population will surely stand out in ways both good and bad. We chose good. As the human resources leader at the University of Colorado at Boulder (CU-Boulder), I treated the custodians and food service workers in the same manner that I treated the Nobel award-winning biochemist, dean, or chancellor. To me, character, not color—and certainly not money or position—defines a person. When I was recognized in 2007 as one of the Women Who Make a Difference at CU-Boulder, I was humbled and honored that my colleagues recognized my spirit and respected my work.

Recently I read a CNN article written by Daniel Burke, CNN religion editor, regarding Jason Denney, a retired Air Force colonel who was gravely ill with COVID-19. Mr. Denney received his last rites and had basically given up on life. That is, until Rosaura Quinteros, the housekeeper responsible for his room, saved his life (his words). The housekeeper was born in Guatemala and spoke English as a second language. She would talk to him and compassionately encourage him daily as she cleaned his room. Language was not a barrier. No one was watching. Before the pandemic, housekeepers were expected to be "invisible" and, like other service or frontline employees, most were not valued.

> *Our healthcare workers are in danger*
> *These heroes are at risk*
> *The frontline staff who weren't valued*
> *Essentially cannot be dismissed.*

> —Excerpt from "Spiritual Reset"

During the pandemic, housekeepers were designated as essential and became highly regarded as crucial to the healing of COVID-19 patients. At this particular hospital, the chaplain manager provided talking points to the staff who entered hospital rooms daily. They were instructed to engage and uplift severely ill and highly contagious patients who spent their time in isolation and fear. Rosaura Quinteros dutifully complied—and saved Mr. Denney's life!

> *Continue not to see me,*
> *Not to look,*
> *But you can't ignore my impact.*
> *When my work is done,*
> *You'll see.*

> —Excerpt from "Invisible Strength"

I was moved by this beautiful story; it echoes messages found in my writing. Three of my poems are reflected in this one story: "What Matters," "Invisible Strength" (written in 2004 prior to my retirement), and "Spiritual Reset" (written April 2020 to describe our grim circumstances during the Spring). Undeniably, COVID-19 exposed the ills of our country. As it triggered the spiritual reset, constructive social change could no longer be deferred.

Personally, I am disheartened yet encouraged. As the world slowed down and the outside noise got quieter, my inner voice became louder! I have written poems for forty-plus years, poems of joy, pain, and general observations. I tended to react quietly to social issues in the past, but now that my inner voice is unleashed, I must continue to write and to share. Words matter. If one story can embody points found in three of my poems, imagine how a book of poems might resonate with millions of stories around the globe. Imagine our world when people have clarity and are willing to respectfully engage with each other. Imagine the social healing, the worldwide spiritual reset.

The aforementioned poems are included in *Poetic Forecast*, a poetry collection I published in 2020. My goal is to inspire others to assess their way of thinking . . . to know what matters. This is how I want my grandchildren and their future grandchildren to live, modeling the values of their great-great-grandmother. I want them to know how I viewed the world during these tumultuous times, and to know what I did to make a difference.

In closing, let's look within ourselves and reach out to others with empathy and an open mind. History and our own experience have shown us that we are resilient. Together we will rise and live as God intended!

Zaneta Varnado Johns is a retired human resources leader and bestselling author. Her twenty-nine-year career was spent at the University of Colorado. A devoted wife, mother, and grandmother, Zan's goal is to touch the world line by line through written creative expression. Her book of insightful poems, Poetic Forecast, *was released in 2020.*

www.zanexpressions.com

THE VISION OF HOPE INSPIRES

Steff Kawasaki

Four expressionless investigators wearing imposing dark suits glared at me across the large rectangular conference table. Three-ring binders and papers of various colors covered the conference table, all meticulously stacked. As I glanced around the room, an intruding video camera with a spotlight blinded me, and a large fuzzy microphone was jammed in my face. A laptop in a metal case with several electronic pieces of equipment was lined up next to index cards labeled with letters and numbers. An operator hunched behind the laptop as if she was embarrassed by technically exploiting me.

Two armed guards stood before each door, fingers poised against rifle triggers. Each had tinted glasses that prevented me from seeing their eyes. I felt their stares pierce through me as if they were trying to read my mind. At that moment the heat of the spotlight felt like it ignited a flame deep within my soul; soon, electrical currents were jolting in my head while a sudden flood of sweat started to drip behind my neck and down my back. The heat in my head made my hair feel hot; it was as though I were wilting in a sauna. My eyes strained as I focused on the room's details. My thoughts scampered chaotically. *Why am I here, and what went wrong?*

I used multiple protocols that protected critical information required in my secured building. I was the conscientious employee, respectful of others, productive, a recipient of numerous performance awards, and the ideal team member. At this moment, however, none of that mattered. The chief investigator read a page of accusations against me primarily for disobeying the order that jeopardized the lives of several people. He read the charges aloud like a robot, with no emotion, no heart, and he didn't even look at me. I was terrified, but I knew this was all a misunderstanding, and there was a logical answer that would leave us all laughing—or so I thought. Taking a deep breath, I confidently looked in the four investigators' eyes, prepared with all the details and knowing that they were sorely mistaken. In a split second, doubts scrolled through my head. *How could I prove my innocence? What if they don't believe me?* I froze with fright, thinking that I couldn't correct this misunderstanding. If I could not confidently deliver my facts, I faced serious consequences. My lips were paralyzed, but the few words that I managed to say were garbled. I stuttered, which made me sound guilty.

The room's silence seemed deafeningly loud. Everyone began whispering among themselves; they seemed to ignore me as if I didn't even exist. The chief investigator nodded to the guards, which drew my attention. I panicked. Immediately, each rifle pointed, one at my head and the other at my heart. *Bang!* I screamed and bolted upright in my bed, my eyes wide open in the total darkness of my bedroom. For a moment I thought I was dead, but my heart was pounding, and my neck and pillow were sopping wet.

It may have been a nightmare, but that was how I lived my life, frozen with the fear of freely expressing my opinion, even if it would save my life. As a child, I lived under the impression that I did not have anything substantial to say. I thought that if I didn't speak fast enough, no one would listen. As a young adult, how well I communicated shaped my significance and self-worth. I often floundered to simultaneously organize my thoughts while trying to speak. It boiled down to the fear of people's thoughts about me. Did I measure up to a standard of smartness? Did I sound intelligent? I often took the safe route by listening instead of participating in discussions, fearing that my ideas would not be received well.

That nightmare was a pivotal moment in my life. *Was I willing to live my best, most purposeful life regardless of what others thought of me?* I realized I had jeopardized many people's lives because I withheld thoughts, informed opinions, and opportunities to engage. Perhaps it wasn't *all about me* and what I lacked. Could I have missed opportunities for sharing perspectives and inspiring others?

I needed to take action and readjust my focus inwardly to be effective outwardly. It had to start with the alignment of my head and my heart. I began a journey of investing in myself. I pursued God like there was no tomorrow and reinforced the foundations of my Christian faith. I knew God had designed me for a purpose, and I sought my authentic identity and the value He created within me. I joined two local Toastmasters International clubs to learn how to speak with confidence and to listen purposefully. I discovered my natural communication style. According to the Fascination Advantage® system, my primary Advantage is *Passion* and my secondary Advantage is *Innovation*; my Archetype is the *Catalyst*.

I recognized many areas where I need refinement, and that's an ongoing process; but I decided that "to sound intelligent" isn't one of them. I communicate with enthusiasm, emotion, creativity, have a growth mindset, and live with an optimistic outlook. Ultimately, I am uniquely brilliant! Since embarking on this journey, the most amazing thing happened: God sent the right people at the right time to cross my path. Each, brilliant in their unique way, played a role in planting a vision of hope and inspired me to live beyond myself and for the benefit of others.

When the vision of hope inspires one person,
imagine the impact of many.

I learned who I am, the value I have, and the necessity of inspiring hope in the world around me. We must continue to live our best selves because whatever we do makes a difference in the world around us. As the journey continues, I will love God, live my purpose on purpose, be blessed, and be a blessing to others.

Steff Kawasaki brings creative energy and fresh ideas to facilitate a culture of engagement in homes, communities, and workplaces. She is a Fascinate Certified Advisor™, Lean Six Sigma Black Belt, and Hope Inspired Coaching founder. As an onscreen actor, she finds joy through character development and sharing stories that inspire hope in humanity.

www.hopeinspiredcoaching.com

A Heroine's Story

Mary E. Knippel

What's more important than being the heroine in your own story?

Well, let's think about that for a minute. What is more important than being the heroine in your own story? Being the heroine in someone else's story! Even better, being the heroine in a lot of someone else's stories!

This chapter is either a loving reminder or a startling revelation of your status.

A heroine is a warrior who leads with her heart. She fights with courage and conviction for herself and others to be able to live life to the fullest.

There are so many ways you already show up as a heroine for yourself and others that you don't even realize. Heroines exist in the here and now, not only "once upon a time" in fairy tales.

In mythology and folklore, a heroine was one whose deeds were the subject of ancient Greek myths. She was a woman of superhuman qualities and often semidivine origin. I'm not suggesting that you go around in a red cape like Superwoman. What I am suggesting is that you concentrate on using your superpowers of compassion, understanding, and intuition in your day-to-day dealings with the world. If we all did this, everyone we encountered would be a little bit better for having crossed our path. Perhaps a little happier. Perhaps a little more hopeful. Perhaps a little more optimistic about meeting life's challenges.

Wondering if you have ever encountered a heroine? I'm sure you have. She may have been saintly like Mother Teresa; a rebel like George Sand; someone you loved who died too young; someone you admire for their guts; someone who challenges you to be your authentic self; or someone you only have a sense of and have yet to meet.

For the location and description of the closest heroine, I direct you to look in the mirror.

Would you trade your ordinary life for that of a superhero? Well, no. I wouldn't. What I would do is savor the myriad of ways someone living an ordinary life full of grace and compassion has an extraordinary impact on the world. Think about a beautiful tapestry and the thousands of strands of thread woven in a precise pattern to produce a work of art. What if you thought of your story as a thread in that design woven into the universal story? You and I each have an individual heroine story which is important to us. Our stories make up an integral part in the universal story.

You become a heroine the minute you are born. It's in our female nature to care about others. It's when we start doubting our instincts to lean into compassion that we lose our innate ability to be the heroine in our own story as well as the heroine in someone else's story.

Too often we grow up and become afraid that we aren't enough. That we will never measure up to the accomplishments of others. We decide that the answer is to play it safe and stay silent. To live invisible and small.

What if *you* decided to be the heroine who faced her fears? Sometimes life demands that you step into your heroine persona when you are the most vulnerable. When your inner critic is shouting, "How could you possibly do that?" and your heart is urging you to take the leap. While a fictional heroine could have a perfectly scripted "happily ever after," it's up to you and me to rewrite our stories to create the outcomes we seek. It's up to us to save ourselves. You and I are the heroines in our own stories and in one another's stories.

Did you ever notice how it takes something really big in your life to make changes? I thought I was leading the life I had always dreamed of having. My husband had a good job, we adopted a sweet baby girl, and life was beautiful. I achieved my goal of earning a college degree and worked part-time as an editorial assistant for a monthly newspaper.

Then the form letter arrived saying I had had an abnormal mammogram. And a second one arrived three years later with the same big red X. My life was never the same again.

I was forced to stop and pause. Has that ever happened to you? Was there ever a time where you ignored whispers to slow down, take a breath, or linger a while? The whisper turned into a howling that would not go away until you paid attention. That nagging feeling of something important will not be put off. And life as you know it changes in an instant.

I woke up to be the heroine in my life after my second surgery. I saw all the ways I was playing it safe and being invisible.

I stepped into leadership roles in the clubs and organizations I participated in. I sought out ways to contribute my skills by volunteering to write articles and use my creativity on newsletters or on fundraising projects. I started speaking and facilitating workshops focusing on the importance of our stories. I was willing to step forward and share more of my voice and story and help others do the same. I became willing to be the heroine in someone else's story.

The most valuable advice I can share with you about discovering your heroine's story is to pick up a pen and write (longhand) in a journal. It's the most incredible tool to be able to connect your heart with your head and literally see your thoughts on the page. Whether you ever want to share those words with the world or just keep a journal for your eyes only, it is important that you gain the insights and wisdom of your inner knowing.

Are you willing to be the heroine in your own story? Where are you perhaps hiding—where are you playing it safe? Where can you step out a little bit more and share more of yourself and your gifts?

Mary E. Knippel is a catalyst for those who are blocked in writing and want to find the freedom to know they have the ability to write, to have compassion for their struggle, and to give themselves permission to recognize that now is the time to let their creativity shine.

www.yourwritingmentor.com

Resilience against Stereotypes

Paula M. Kramer

The day I was born, my mother stereotyped me as a threat. I was her second daughter instead of her first son. My mentally ill immigrant grandmother had raised my mother and her older sister to believe they could prove themselves worthy women only as mothers of sons.

To protect herself from the threat my mother saw in me, she tried to kill me twice. My father was away from home for each attempt. I buried my murder secret memories until I was forty-two years old.

When my mother failed to murder me physically, she spent the rest of my childhood doing her best to murder me mentally and emotionally. She also protected herself from the threat of me talking about the murder attempts. She taught relatives and neighbors to ignore what I said and discount what I did. My siblings learned their lessons so well that they began treating me like a trespasser in their lives.

When I was twelve years old, a boy in school pulled my chair out from under me. I landed hard on my tailbone and my spine started hurting. Medical professionals misdiagnosed my spinal injury for thirty-three years. Some of them stereotyped me as whiny or hostile. The pain kept increasing. Normal sitting and standing became especially painful. My mother and siblings discounted my injury and ignored my pain. I finally reached a point where I felt I had to end my relationship with my mother.

At twenty-six years old, I got married. At twenty-seven years old, my husband and I had a baby girl. Then, when I was twenty-eight years old, my husband died suddenly. I became a disabled single parent. A number of people stereotyped me as hiding behind my child and looking for free handouts when I needed financial help. "Freeloader me" should just go out and get a job. Never mind that normal sitting and standing left me in extreme pain.

I didn't go to college when I graduated high school because my mother wanted to control my college and career choices. I considered going to college after my husband died, but remembering all of the stereotypes against me, I thought American society would not allow me to succeed in college. I still did what I could to end stereotypes for others.

I wrote letters to the editor frequently for about nine years, repeatedly writing about poverty and hunger. A friend of mine was in a babysitting co-op. At one meeting, a woman asked if anyone knew Paula Kramer. My friend said she knew me. The woman asked, "Is Paula fat and does she sit in front of the TV set all day eating potato chips?" My friend set the woman straight.

After one letter about poverty and hunger, I received a phone call. The woman caller asked if I was the Paula Kramer who wrote letters to the editor. Not knowing what to expect, I said yes. The woman asked, "Is there anything I can do to help?" Over the next year or so, that family spoke positive words to me and occasionally made my life easier. I listened to that family and decided I could go to college and succeed. I began college at age thirty-five. I now have two degrees.

When I took Communication 101, I was one of two nontraditional students in the class. I considered the other nontrad student the best speaker in the class. After one of my speeches, the other nontrad student approached me to ask what my grade had been on that speech. I said it was A-. The other student said, "You'd think you and I could get straight As." I listened to what she said and decided to become a professional speaker.

When I was forty-five, I finally heard the correct diagnosis for my spinal injury. At the beginning of a talk to a businesswomen's group, I told the audience about my injury to explain my using a tall stool instead of standing. I asked the audience to tell any children in their lives to never pull a chair out from under anyone. A nurse came up afterward to give me the correct diagnosis and treatment. When I landed hard on my tailbone, my spinal cord tensed up. As the tension in my spinal cord increased, my pelvis continually shifted backward until I had no S curve in my spine. A spine without an S curve finds normal sitting and standing extremely painful. After thirty-three years of misdiagnoses, the treatment the nurse suggested worked, and the pain in my spine finally ended.

As a child, I listened to anyone who said positive words to me—my father, my teachers, my friends. I learned to say positive words to myself.

As an adult I continue listening to positive words from friends, coworkers, neighbors, supervisors, and strangers. I speak positive words to people of all ages and descriptions.

My grandparents' first child was a boy who died in infancy. My mother was the second daughter who was supposed to be a son. My mother and aunt did not have a loving father saying positive words to them. Their paranoid schizophrenic mother threatened their father with a butcher knife. He left the family to save his own life. My mother and aunt grew up with their mother's soul-crushing stereotype. Their youth provided few other positive words, and my mother did not learn to say positive words to herself.

After I ended my relationship with my mother, my aunt sent me Christmas cards for the rest of her life. We had not exchanged cards before because my mother discouraged family connections to protect her secrets. Those cards meant that my aunt had learned to say positive words to herself.

My mother continued the stereotype her mother forced on her because she didn't have the resilience to rise up against it. Listening to and speaking positive words, I rose up against my mother's stereotype and the stereotypes of everyone else who tried to force failure on me. My positive words to other people bring unexpected benefits into my life, renewing my own resilience.

Paula M. Kramer has researched stereotypes since 1988. Using her degrees in Women's Studies and Communication, she conducts online workshops for ending stereotypes in negative workplace gossip and for chipping away stereotypes that build glass ceilings for anyone. All of Paula's recommended strategies use positive words and actions.

www.speakingfromtriumph.com

Follow the Pebbles

Lorraine Lane

When I was growing up, "Do your best" translated into work hard, study hard, bring home A's on your report card, but most of all, don't get into trouble. I carried this "head down and work hard" approach into my work life and it paid off—until it didn't.

I joined a high-tech company as a recruiter and excelled, but I wasn't satisfied and wanted to achieve real mastery. That led me to jump at the opportunity to learn from Barry, the company's top recruiter. But my initial delight came to an end after only two months when Barry announced that he was leaving to start his own agency.

My well-crafted plan had fallen apart. Barry was replaced with the only other woman in our department of twelve recruiters, and I was given my new manager's old assignment consisting of the hardest jobs to fill, some of which had been open for months. My assistant and I worked hard and creatively to fill them, and we succeeded. The delighted hiring managers wrote letters of appreciation to Pauline, my new manager. She never shared them with me, but I learned of them accidentally. She viewed my success as showing her up, while in my mind, I was just "doing my best" to do my job.

Performance review time came, and because I was filling openings in record time and hiring managers were praising my work, I expected a decent, if not glowing, review. Instead, Pauline was critical and disapproving. She complained that I didn't manage my time well and wasn't a team player.

Our rating scale was 1–5: a 1 meant you had better start a job search, while a 5 rang out that you were a star. I was rated a 2 with no raise. I was stunned. I refused to sign the review—a company requirement. I didn't agree.

That night, after I read my daughter, Elizabeth, a bedtime story and kissed her good night, I made a life-changing decision. I could not let my little girl down. I was her only supportive parent, and I had to step up and find my voice. I would not accept this review and let it be okay. Because it wasn't. I worked through the night and wrote a rebuttal showcasing my work. It felt strange to be bragging about my accomplishments, but who else would stand up for me? I still remember how alone I felt that night. One minute I was as mad as hell, and the next minute I was bawling because I had to defend myself. The torturous minutes became hours, and I kept writing and rewriting until it was time to get Elizabeth and myself ready for the day.

I brought my rebuttal to Donna, the division director and Pauline's manager. She proceeded to arrange a three-way meeting, during which she argued the case for a re-review taking into account what the managers had written about my performance.

Astonishingly, Pauline refused to reconsider: "The review stands as written." To save me from further suffering from this manager, I was assigned to a "special project" with Brian M. Anyone on a "special project" was considered to be a short timer, a person who wasn't going to make it.

But instead, what happened was that Brian gave me a *real* project. The division had been surveyed a few years earlier, and a new survey was conducted to see if the remedies had any effect on morale. My job was to organize focus groups and present the survey findings, which allowed me to meet all the managers in the division. Additionally, I learned to analyze the data to reveal additional insight. The deep dive into this work took my mind off the horrific performance review and demonstrated to management my ability to organize and step up to a challenge.

Soon Brian asked me to take a high-level position in Field Service headquarters, which opened the door to the next eight years of my career—an opportunity I would never have had if Pauline had not rated me a 2! In retrospect, I'm grateful for that 2, though it's taken me a long time to have true appreciation. What I learned:

- To stand up for myself and refuse to be a victim of others' opinions. This has served me when I've coached professionals to stand up and speak up. It sometimes takes nerves of steel.
- Asking for help takes courage. Taking my rebuttal to Donna and asking for her help felt like the longest walk. Since then, I've had to learn over and over again that asking for help is not an admission of failure, but rather an opportunity to connect with the power of "seek and you will find."

- Build relationships! It's the most important part of any job! As a high achiever, I can work head-down without coming up for air. I didn't build a relationship with Pauline. I didn't see her as an important part of my job. This was very wrong thinking. While self-sufficiency might be commendable, when it's overdone, it deprives you and others of the joy of connection and collaboration.
- Step Up, Step Over, Step Into. While it might sound cliché, when one door closes, another opens. Opening your mind, heart, and arms to what is ahead helps heal what has happened in the past. Throwing yourself into a new opportunity can catapult you into the next thing in ways you can't now imagine.

It took me a long time to heal from Pauline's caustic review, but I've since learned and accepted that it was a good thing. It was a Divine intervention I could not have planned for myself. I often coach my clients to "follow the pebbles in the road." The road we walk is often strewn with pebbles that we kick aside. Before you do the kicking, pay attention. Is this a pebble that needs your attention?

Lorraine Lane inspires her business clients to step into their leadership roles. In her work as a corporate trainer, her clients develop their strengths, skills, and insights. Lorraine is a speaker, consultant, and author and serves as the global business connector for Women Speakers Association in Tampa, Florida.

www.lanebc.com

Strength beyond Stress and Mental Illness

Catherine M. Laub

I've fallen, cried, been angry and afraid, but even when I was hurting, I always found a way to keep going. *A strong woman never gives up.*

My history of mental illness is familiar to all that know me. My angels guided me to share the details and inspire others to attain support. My slogan is "Brighten Your Day with Turquoise." Turquoise is a calming color and creates emotional balance and stability.

2019 began with a lot of promise. At a business event, I read one of my stories on stage, and it was filmed as a marketing tool.

February began the collapse and was spent with my mother until she died on March 24th. She had cancer but caught C. diff in the hospital. Tony, my husband, drove her to her appointments and also caught C. diff. He became ill on Easter Sunday, and then on May 5th, he was diagnosed with colon cancer. I was devastated, even though as a psychic, I had predicted his death the year before. I was supportive, but I knew he would not survive.

We prepared my mother's house to sell and agreed to bring many belongings to my house. I sorted and donated most of them. It was hard work, and on May 16th, I developed Broken Heart Syndrome due to all the stress and strenuous physical activity. This is called *Takotsubo cardiomyopathy*, where I lost a lot of heart function.

While in the hospital, my daughters lectured me about the amount of "stuff" in my house, and this caused additional and unnecessary stress.

Father's Day 2019 was the worst. My daughter walked in and went on a rant. "OMG, Mommy, you are sick! You can't have all this stuff here! It's not fair to Tony!" Tony had agreed to bring the stuff here but then agreed with her. I continued to sort the "stuff," even though my energy was low. Later

Tony and I fought, and he lectured me, so I shut down. I started throwing things because I was frustrated. Most of the night I chanted: "Nobody loves me, and I'm a piece of sh**."

This behavior was not new. I have several mental illnesses and have been hospitalized multiple times since 2003. The next day my doctors decided I needed a break, so I was hospitalized for two weeks. I inspired many of the other patients with my negative stories and how I overcame them every time. I shared my book with three patients, and they were amazed with all I had been through and overcame.

In October of 2019, my daughter had the police come to pick me up because I was suicidal. The day before Tony's daughter had threatened me. I told her I would not allow her to talk to me that way. Then Tony yelled at me for being insecure. He did not listen appropriately. I stormed out and became suicidal.

I did not want to go with the police because I was helping Tony with his daily healthcare. But they could have taken me against my will. Another week was spent in the hospital, and Tony was left alone to care for himself.

My mental illnesses have caused considerable friction at times with family members. They do not understand the reason for some of the things I say when I have bipolar episodes.

Tony declined quickly and died on February 25, 2020. He went to hospice in one ambulance and another ambulance took me to the hospital. I thought I had time to see Tony before he died, but didn't. I was extremely erratic—passing out several times, hallucinating, and apparently very nasty, so I needed answers. There was a steady flow of people in my house, and they had no concern for my privacy. They said I did not matter—that it was all about Tony. This caused me to become extremely anxious. As an empath, I didn't realize at the time that I was absorbing the negative energy.

I had been taking an anti-anxiety medication, which we later realized caused my symptoms. The week before Tony died, I was in the psych ward for three days because the medication was making me suicidal. When I returned home, I was not allowed to be alone with Tony because his stepdaughter said I was going to hurt him! I am haunted by the horror of that week.

I am on disability, and it does not cover much. My psychic readings stopped, so I realized I would need to sell my house. I began to pack, which caused another episode of Broken Heart Syndrome. I have heart failure and am categorized as at risk for sudden death.

I promote psychic readings by posting "Are you feeling alone and need to talk to someone that you miss?" However, because of the pandemic, the economy is producing no responses.

After I lost Tony, my depression lifted. I realized that being an empath caused my prominent mental illnesses. We fought, and I stormed out frequently. Our marriage counselor suggested that I walk away during a fight to cool down. But Tony followed me and only caused more frustration. I realize now that he never really listened to me, so he did not understand why I was upset.

There hasn't been much happiness in my life for a while. I'm positive, though, that my move will begin a new and better chapter.

When I experience setbacks, I struggle to get through, but I always persevere! Without the negative events, I can't understand others. My angels gave me the mission to help others with mental illness and stress many years ago, and I am told by many that my story is powerful. I love helping others and guiding them through my psychic readings.

During the COVID-19 pandemic, many people were isolated, including me. Many of us have struggled through the stress of loneliness. Some committed suicide, and others contemplated it. We must work together to keep everyone's spirits high, so we can all find peace for a better future.

You are not alone, and there is a support system waiting for you.

*Recently widowed, **Catherine M. Laub** hosts her self-produced podcast* The Celestial Spoon, *is an award-winning inspirational author, speaker, psychic/medium, spiritual guide, and advocate for mental illness. She guides people to understand they can live with illness and still have a happy life.*

www.catherinemlaub.com

DID YOU SAY SCHOOL AT MY AGE?

Anne McAwley-LeDuc, RN, APRN

*Maybe now it's time to start
That dream held tight within your heart.*

What am I doing, trudging across the expansive campus of this rural university in the frigid cold? I am totally lost and not a soul in sight to help me with directions. This is called a "walking" campus. I hadn't realized that, without benches, you walk and walk until your legs buckle beneath you. Okay, maybe I'm not in the greatest shape. I wince as my boot hits a small rock embedded in the ground—the ugly brown ground. A blanket of fresh snow would make this trek less gloomy.

The beauty of a quintessential New England church steeple in the distance is lost through the tears freezing on my face. I am an experienced registered nurse (RN) making a good salary. Do I really want to put myself through a grueling educational experience at age fifty-one? Do I really want to go back to school at my age? Yes—so I push on.

Sometime later, exhausted and totally numb from the cold, I find the nursing school. My frozen spirits start to thaw as I start my path to become a nurse practitioner (APRN).

I learned two lessons that day: remember the dream when the going gets tough and buy warmer boots!

Fast-forward three years from that frigid first day of school. I easily stroll across the university's sprawling grounds, smiling because I am headed to my last class and I have dropped ten pounds from frequently crisscrossing this "walking" campus. A blanket of lush green grass covers the ground. The beauty of that New England church steeple in the distance is not lost through the few tears of joy that mist my eyes. I did it! I graduate with honors and enjoy my new career as a nurse practitioner for nearly a decade.

You might be asking, "Did you say 'school at my age'?" I sure did! School is simply learning. What's your dream—obtaining a GED high school diploma, learning a second language, getting a college degree, earning a job-specific certification? What mode fits your life circumstances—a traditional university, online courses, an adult education program, or a book self-study? It's all learning—it's all school. Don't forget a fun hobby class—that's the best school of all!

How do you know when it's time to go for it? You think it in your mind, and you feel it in your heart. Your life circumstances allow you to try. You may need to tweak your goal to one that is attainable, one that can still be very rewarding.

From a young age, I had always wanted to be a nurse. So after high school, off to nursing school I went. My first job as a registered nurse was in orthopedics, and I still recall walking down the hospital hall in my white uniform and nursing cap, saying to myself, "This is so much fun!"

At age fifty I was walking down the hall of a different hospital in my colored scrubs, bringing medication to a patient. I clearly remember saying to myself, "I don't want to give pills to patients anymore; I want to order them for patients." I absolutely knew in my heart that this was the moment for a career change—it was time to become a nurse practitioner, and I never looked back.

Are you still on the fence about school and wondering, "Do I still have what it takes?" Do you cringe at the thought of tests and break into a sweat over writing formal papers again?

As an older student, studying was different, and yes, it was harder. For years I tried to hide from the computer, but school forced me into the modern era, and I learned to love the cut-and-paste function. Obstacles popped up requiring compromise and sacrifice. But that's life, right? Older students embrace the whole experience differently and it becomes fun—even writing those papers—and I have seen many get the best grades! I'm here to tell you, "You can do this!"

Learning opportunities come in all sizes and shapes. A full-time university program happened to fit my needs when I went back to school. I have a friend who obtained a Bachelor of Arts degree after high school and worked in social services. Years later, pursuing her passion and talent, she went to art school part-time while continuing her full-time job. She now teaches art classes.

Another friend did not get a college degree, but instead she completed a difficult self-study course with national exams that earned her the designation of Chartered Property Casualty Underwriter (CPCU), which is the highest designation in the insurance industry.

These friends chose different types of "school" and both completed their "older" educational endeavors when they were forty-two years old.

So when are you too old to go back to school? Never! Scan the headlines and you will find ninety-nine-year-olds to one hundred-plus-year-olds completing college degrees. A 101-year-old man completed his bachelor's degree. A ninety-four-year-old woman finished her bachelor's degree with intentions to go on for her master's degree. Both accomplished their dreams through online courses.

If school is your dream . . . go for it. Enjoy the journey of learning . . . at any age!

So many of our dreams at first seem impossible, then improbable, and then, when we summon the will, they soon become inevitable.
CHRISTOPHER REEVE

Anne McAwley-LeDuc, RN, APRN, believes: "Dream it, go for it . . . no matter what your age!" A retired nurse practitioner, she now writes and speaks on health-related topics. Media appearances include TV, radio, and podcasts. Her first book, *Personal Health Organizer,* won an international award in the caregiving category.

www.personal-health-organizer.com

THE ANIMALS ARE COMMUNICATING WITH YOU—ARE YOU LISTENING?

Chiara Marrapodi

I was drawn to animals from a very young age. My heart leapt with joy as I watched them move through time and space. I observed as they savored every movement, every moment. They were fully immersed in their environment—it was the type of immersion I longed for because it allowed them to be fully present. I noticed the light in their eyes, a sign of aliveness. I realized early on that I, the observer, was being observed. They were watching me as closely as I was watching them. They watched me as though they could see me. But it was more than just observation. It was an intense understanding of who I was, in the blink of an eye. The animals saw me. I felt bare, vulnerable. They tapped deep into the parts of me I wanted to hide. But being vulnerable is such a great teacher, and the feeling was soon replaced by a sense of being heard, seen, and accepted. I started to feel comfortable. I was trusted, and I could trust in return. My heart lit up. It felt warm . . . full. I felt joy, an immense joy. When I was two years old, wild birds spontaneously landed in my lap and in my hands, but only later did I begin to understand and articulate the feelings I experienced.

You see, what I have learned over the years is that when we connect with animals in a deeply coherent way, we are connecting with parts of our own selves. A beautiful tortoiseshell feline named Smudge came into my life many years ago and taught me that animals are a deep part of who we are. When we connect with a domestic animal for a length of time, we meld with them energetically, and they begin to reflect parts of who we are. They literally enmesh with us and act as our support line.

I've learned that animals are conscious. They have emotions and thoughts. They sense more than we can imagine. They have an internal reality. They can see deep inside our hearts. This is why animals know what we need; it's why they can change our lives. They change the way we see ourselves and how we feel about our human experience. They open our hearts and minds. They ease the pain and hold us up when we feel down. They shine the light back into our hearts. This is their purpose in life. It's a purpose they take very seriously.

They do this so well because of their uncanny ability to connect with us. Animals connect with their whole selves. I call this deep connectivity. Deep connectivity involves deep listening. This type of listening involves connecting with their bodies, minds, and hearts. When animals deeply listen to humans, they lighten our load. Indeed, they are so devoted to their humans that they often give more than they can bear. They are known to sacrifice their own vitality to support their humans. For thousands of years, their actions have changed the course of humanity, individually and collectively. Animals are selflessly devoted, and without them our evolution would be stunted.

With this in mind, my invitation to all humanity is a calling for a deeper connectivity with animals. The animals have been teaching me this since I was two years old. It is my purpose and passion to now teach this connectivity to all humans who are ready to deepen their relationships with their animals. Animals use all their senses, their full body, and the purity of their hearts. Animals read you emotionally, physically, and energetically, and therefore you cannot hide from them. They know more than you think they do. They share of themselves and their essence using their eyes, bodies, and interactions. The human-animal bond is based on connection. And connection is an invitation to explore truth—a truth silently whispered between beings. These whispers are subtle, yet they are a powerful way to share an unspoken, sacred language. It's a language that enriches the human experience if we allow ourselves to receive it in its true form. It is the sacred dialogue from one heart to another.

So the next time you are with your animal, release any ideas, thoughts, and human projections you hold about who they are and their motivations. This is referred to as anthropomorphism, and it is common in the animal-human bond experience. Perhaps you did not notice that you were projecting human traits and ideas upon them. These projections are barriers to deeply experiencing and knowing animals on their own terms. Seeing them from their perspective is the greatest gift any human can bestow on them. To be seen, to be heard, to be understood—this is love in its purest form. It is the way toward the true connection you are seeking with your animal family and inevitably with yourself.

This simple exercise begins your animal-connectivity practice:

Let any ideas, thoughts, and human projections drop to the ground.
Focus your attention on your heart space and imagine breathing in and out of the heart center.
As you do so, notice when you begin to feel stillness.
In the stillness and calm, send an imaginary golden thread from your heart to your animal's heart.
Slow your breath, be still, and notice what this feels like.
This is the beginning of what I call the animal-human heart connection.

The heart is the gateway to life-changing experiences and perceptions. Remember when you fell in love for the first time? It was surreal. It was not just a rush of chemicals from your brain to the body; it was intertwined with tentacles from your heart. Animals activate the coherence of the heart, allowing you to sense, feel, and experience life differently in the present moment. When you listen to the animals, they share themselves fully with you. They share their minds, emotions, and lives. There is no purer gift between beings than the shared heart space. It aligns you with your true essence.

Chiara Marrapodi is a clinical hypnotherapist and life transitions advisor. She is the founder of the Society for Animal Consciousness and also specializes in animal connectivity and trauma. A 2015/2016 Bernard Grad Emerging Scientist, Chiara is well known for her transformational education programs.

www.chiaramarrapodi.com

April's Rain

Toni Martin

I grew up in a typical dysfunctional American-Sicilian family. Life revolved around the very loud kitchen. Coffee was always brewing, and Mom was always cooking. We moved to Florida when I was nine and quickly became known as the crazy neighborhood Italian family.

I have two older brothers. One is a handsome guitar player, and the other is a gladiator who loved sports and girls. I, on the other hand, was living proof that God has a sense of humor—a quirky little girl with an afro, a unibrow, and a mustache. This, coupled with my awkward skinniness and pimply face, made me a real sight for sore eyes. Surely the mullet with bangs trimmed around my hairline took attention away from my unibrow and sideburns, right? I mean, why wouldn't any skinny, hairy girl with a "boy's name" feel alluring and confident like her older brothers?

My mom: Loved to cook. Bad temper. Could turn anything into a weapon—all you had to do was place an object near her. Spoons, toys, purses all meant ninja. If she threw her shoe at you, you'd better believe it would follow you around corners.

Our parents fostered children for thirty years on and off—from little kids to teenagers. Mom's street-savvy edge gave her a natural understanding for the hardened teens living with us. If they smoked, she'd happily share her cigarettes. When they cried, she held them.

I grew angry that I had to share my parents, brothers, room, and life with foster kids. Uncomfortable in my own house, I never stopped to think what it must have been like for them having to move into a stranger's home. My mom would say, "Toni, they have no one." Forced to become siblings with kids who had been dealt the most horrible hands in life, I was too immature to see the lesson behind it.

The teens we took in were hardened, depressed, and untrusting, each coping with their own traumas. One girl watched her mother drown her brother. Another had fork and burn marks on her hands and arms where her mother stabbed and burned her. Sexually abused girls would try to look and dress like boys to protect themselves as a defense mechanism. I've lived with girls who were raped, beaten, and disfigured. Though my family was far from perfect, I can honestly say our home was a safe haven for these foster kids.

While I was going through my petty struggles trying to control my fluffy hair and deal with being picked on, at least I had a mom and dad's support. These girls, on the other hand, literally had *nothing*! They didn't have anyone to protect them. They didn't hear "I love you" and have birthday celebrations or even a real childhood. They were too busy protecting their siblings from rape and caring for them when their parents were high. These girls knew more about the darkness of life than most adults do. Their tough exterior, however, never discouraged my mother for one second. She was a tough cookie herself and had a natural kinship with them. I heard about her fistfights, how she beat her cousin with a bat, and how she had been chased by her mother with a hatchet at fourteen for smoking! To my mother, the foster girls were lost sheep like she once was.

I was this skinny girl who had trouble making friends, and these girls gave me a sisterhood. Sometimes we fought with each other. Many times we laughed. I'll never forget one girl in particular; I'll call her April. She came to us as a teen with her sisters. She was tough as nails and very protective of her siblings. Abused by men for years, she decided to identify as a tough man. Eventually she became my best friend, though. She accepted me and never made fun of me the way other people did.

April and my mother had a very strong connection. As their closeness grew, I became increasingly threatened and jealous. Afraid that Mom would love her and not me, I became cruel. This selfish, shortsighted behavior still haunts me to this day. I couldn't see at twelve what I understand now at forty. April eventually moved away, but she kept in touch with my mom by phone.

My mom passed away due to a combination of COPD and lung cancer a few years ago. As she grew ill and was bedridden, she always looked forward to her Sunday calls with April. Today I keep in touch with April, and I tell her I love her as often as possible. Though I've apologized, I can't help but wonder if she might have had a better life or believed in herself more if I had been kinder. It took years for me to forgive myself and realize I was just a kid who didn't know how to cope with emotions.

How many of us women refuse to admit that we have similar childlike emotions within us, preventing us from supporting each other? When did cattiness and gossip become a sign of femininity or strength? We've all seen the glares, the looks, the cold dismissal after an introduction, the unfriendly body language, and the stuck-up facades. What affirmation have we ever seen come from this behavior?

If there is one thing I'd like you to take away from this chapter, it's this: Every woman has a little girl inside of her. Every woman has cried, felt pain, and experienced some past trauma you can't imagine. So don't add one miniscule drop of unwarranted pain to someone else's life. Show that lost, fearful teen inside of you that you are now a strong and confident woman who does not become unhinged by another woman's success, beauty, or status. Instead, become infrangible by supporting other women and helping them succeed.

This writing is dedicated to April, who showed me that true strength is being able to show love to others, even when the world has not shown it to you.

*With a compassion learned from her parents who welcomed foster children into their home for thirty years, **Toni Martin** has a natural desire to truly understand people. Her work and personal life are centered around the building of relationships, and she finds joy in her faith, family, and laughter.*

LOVE IS ROUND

Sherry Morgan

Love, connection, and belonging are birthrights, yet we tend to live with a sense of separation. As I learn, I teach others to tap into that sense of connection experientially. I've waited lifetimes for this opportunity, but that's another story.

I grew up in a fully colonized context, enjoying many comforts but also suffering from a judgmental upbringing. I, too, became judgmental and self-righteous. I argued with anyone who disagreed with me. Underneath my righteousness was a young woman who believed herself fundamentally flawed and unlovable.

In 1982 I had a spiritual calling that set my life on a new trajectory. For the next thirteen years, I felt compelled to pursue personal growth work and spiritual exploration. Following guidance, in 1995 I set out alone from Toronto in a Volkswagen van for a journey of unknown duration and unknown destinations, *knowing* I would be led.

In the fall of that year, I found myself in California, lighting a candle and some incense and declaring in a prayer: "I am ready to do whatever it is I came here to do in this lifetime, and ready to learn whatever lessons I still need to learn in order to do that." For a few days I added: "Well, almost anything." Then one day I felt urged from "somewhere" to drop the conditions.

I met my main teacher, a Huichol indigenous shaman, in Puerto Vallarta, Mexico, a couple of months later, and life became really interesting! In some ways my personal growth work was necessary preparation for the spiritual path I now found myself on, which is when my real learning began.

One year and many experiences later, this teacher assigned me a number of tasks and sent me back to Canada. One of the assignments was to do a vision quest with a minimum three-day fast. I was introduced to an Ojibway elder by the name of Carolyn Oliver who, after a significant process of discernment, agreed to accept my request even though I am a white woman. The vision quest involved four of us. Carolyn provided us with teachings beforehand and had us prepare different offerings. We completed our vision quest in late October 1997, after which I began to receive messages to teach people about prayer. My Huichol teacher called me back to Mexico to begin preparation for this.

The core basis of prayer, I was taught, is the experience of connection with whomever or whatever we engage in prayer. This is in contrast to what I had learned in my childhood when prayers were cast out in hope of being heard. Another principle I learned is that prayer is meant to be more of a conversation than a one-way communication. Wow, I certainly had not experienced an actual conversation with Spirit before!

Or had I? I remembered back to the fall of 1995 when I found myself in prayer declaring: "I am ready . . ."

In 2000, I began teaching people about prayer using the format I had been given. Students began to have what I would call miraculous experiences of connection. Several shed tears of joy as they experienced the love that came pouring back to them. Some shared a state of ecstasy. Many were surprised to experience no separation between themselves and the plant, rock, or tree with which they related. Most were moved by the guidance they received.

Spirit, I learned, is very ready to help us with the guidance we need to walk our path. Receiving guidance is a tremendous benefit of prayer.

One landmark experience I can share is from the late 1990s when I was doing volunteer work for an organization called the Child Abuse Survivor Monument Project. Inspired to find a way to help, I turned to prayer and asked, "What is the one thing I could do to make the biggest difference toward the end of child abuse?" In the next moment I was shaking! I was shown that from my human perspective I cannot know the answer to that question, but Spirit does. I was then shown actions to take that led to finding a major donor, a teacher who created a program to educate children about abuse, and a proposal for a location for the monument.

Both science and spirituality tell us that we are all connected, but how often do we actually experience this connection? Over my years of teaching, I've come to see that restoring our experience of connection, relationship, and sense of belonging in the world is what healing is all about. We heal from the illusion that we are separate. By way of affirmation, I recently discovered a quote from Thich Nhat Hanh: "We are here to awaken from our illusion of separateness."

The words *Love Is Round* arrived with incredible poignancy during my prayers one day in 2015. Love Is Round reveals a core design of our Universe, explains the experience of spiritual connectedness, provides a template for our healing, and has become the context for my work.

The Dalai Lama has expressed surprise at how much self-hatred there is in our culture. The president of Shambhala Buddhism Worldwide has said, "We live in a culture of self-loathing." I spent years experiencing this self-loathing. My twin brother committed suicide because of his self-loathing. When I look out into our world, I see dysfunction everywhere. Do our dysfunctional actions arise out of being lost? Are we lost because we don't know our deeper, worthy selves, or how to access them? Are we in despair because we believe ourselves unlovable?

Regardless of our self-doubt or our deeds, we *are* all loved, and guidance to fulfill our purpose and find our joy *is* accessible.

I would never have guessed that teaching people about prayer would be my life's work, but I am clear that it is what I came here to do. While it may be a very small part of Spirit's overall plan for helping us return to our birthright sense of love and belonging, to me it brings indescribable fulfillment.

Sherry Morgan's insights draw on elders in the Huichol, Náhuatl, and Ojibwa indigenous traditions she has apprenticed with, as well as on direct guidance and experience she has received. She offers public speaking, personal coaching, and workshops that help people open their hearts, fulfill their purpose, and find their joy through effective spiritual prayer.

www.loveisround.net

Rising Against All Odds

Winnie Mwikali

"Mom, you used to be free, happy, and in charge of your own affairs. Are you going to sit there and be sad for yourself or are you going to change things?" my eldest son James asked me.

It had been a few months after we had relocated to another country, and the children were settled in school. I didn't realize that I was depressed from the move. A lot had changed for me. As a CEO, I was now at home without a busy schedule, no longer working on the next strategy to put us ahead of our competitors or meeting with new clients whose lives we transformed. I had been transforming the lives of middle managers. In an industry that was dominated by men, I had made a mark.

I always thought that I could handle whatever life threw at me, but this time I wasn't handling it well. I was losing confidence in the face of the situation and was beginning to lose control over my life. Have you been in such a situation?

It's sometimes hard to notice that you are in such a situation. Sometimes it takes another person to see and identify it for you to realize it. My son was worried, as he had been watching me, but I wasn't aware that I was so affected by being away from my office. The loss of meaning was slowly creeping in, though. Work had given me a sense of meaning, self-esteem, and confidence. I had to find new meaning for my life!

I had many questions. *How would I find meaning in this new set of circumstances? Where should I start? How could I overcome my self-doubt?*

I was in a new environment, and I was lonely when everyone left in the morning. I counted the hours as I waited for the children to come home from school. Confidence can take a hit anywhere. The reality is, without confidence, it's hard to pick yourself up and keep going. Sometimes you just need to deal with the things that hit you.

The first step was acknowledging the emotional impact of what happened.

I was unhappy, lonely, and depressed. The key here was not to wallow in negative emotions. I had to do what I needed to process the situation, and then move on. If you find yourself in a similar situation, ask yourself what you can discover and allow yourself to grow from the experience.

Quitting is the easiest thing in the world to do, especially when your confidence is shattered. How could I restore my confidence and make it impossible to give up?

The local language was the first thing I needed to learn to enable me to communicate and find my way around. Secondly, I needed to find out how I could operate two offices from a home office. I was grateful that my family would support me during this season of change.

I had to find a way to reinvent myself. This situation provided me with an opportunity to rediscover and redefine myself. As the saying goes, when life gives you lemons, make lemonade. I needed to adjust if I was to move forward, and my son's question shocked me into the realization that I was still responsible for how my life would turn out. This was no time to remain a victim of these circumstances.

I realized that what we do affects others around us, and we can never underestimate our impact on others.

It was time to shift gears and change my situation. I tapped into three strategies to move myself from a position of victim to a victor. First, I saw myself as *exceptional*. I had to accept my new reality. When dealing with change, sometimes acceptance is not easy, but unless we do, it's hard to move on. Letting go helped me to accept that I was no longer in the place where I used to be. I couldn't go to the office. I was going to work from home now.

I needed a mindset shift. Being in a place where working from home was unheard of was such a challenge. I had to believe it was possible to manage two offices in two different locations from home.

I was going to remain in control despite my circumstances. My knowledge that I am unique helped me adjust. Once I accepted my new situation, it was time to take action to make it work. I identified what I needed to learn and do to be successful.

Second, I focused on being *extraordinary*. I learned that if I took care of myself, I would be able to take care of those I served. I set up a home office. I came up with a new schedule and routine that I would follow. I signed up for fitness sessions. With this in place, I began taking control of my life and creating a new future for myself.

I went out to meet new people and build strategic relationships with them. I figured out that I could make my new location a destination for our live training. I needed to meet people who could provide that environment for our clients. Seeing this possibility boosted my confidence and initiated the momentum I needed to get moving. If I could give our clients an exciting learning experience, then I would have succeeded at transforming their lives.

If I could work remotely and still create transformation for others, then I could inspire them to overcome what they considered to be their odds. With that spirit in mind, I had to sell the idea to my colleagues.

Third, I was ready to be *excellent* and give excellent service to our clients. Transforming others means moving them from where they are to where they imagine they could be. Most of our clients are middle managers who don't realize their full potential.

When you are confident, you believe in yourself. You have the ability and skills to do what is required of you. You can then inspire others to be the best version of themselves. Always remember, you, too, are exceptional, extraordinary, and excellent.

Winnie Mwikali is a leadership development coach, transformational speaker, and the bestselling author of Shatter Your Glass Ceiling. *Winnie holds a BEd and MBA in Strategic Management. She is the CEO and founder of International Renaissance Centre, where she specializes in coaching her clients on how to unleash their leadership potential.*

www.arcafrica.org

Never Give Up

Susan Owensby

"He loves me; he loves me not. He loves me; he loves me not." As we pull the petals from a flower, we repeat with smiles and frowns these common words. Although I mostly recited this as a child, as I grew older, I said the words and pulled the petals from within my heart. We all crave love, acceptance, and kindness. Are you still awaiting your fairy-tale ending? Do you feel you have made too many poor choices or feel too "stuck" to accomplish your dreams?

When I was a child, I dreamed that one day I would help people, especially women who are hurting from their past. When I went through my divorce, I thought I would never fulfill this vision. Then I realized that the pain and hurts in life do not stop us from accomplishing our dreams; instead they propel us forward to achieve them.

I first married when I was nineteen years old, after graduating high school and attending my first year of college. I watched my older sister get married right out of high school, and I wanted to be just like her. She married the man she went to senior prom with, so I did the same. Besides, I waited a whole year after high school unlike her, so I *knew* I should be ready.

I kept hearing rumors but did not want to believe them. He cheated on me with several women, and he was hooked on pornography, club-hopping, and alcohol. Then came the sexual and verbal abuse, followed by physical abuse. I had to swallow my pride and admit I made a mistake; I never should have married him. It's a hard lesson to learn, but don't do anything in life unless you have complete peace!

The state law at the time was that we had to be separated for one year before the divorce was final. One day during this time he came to my house and started yelling at me. When he threw me against the footboard of the bed, I was in excruciating pain and couldn't move. I ended up in the hospital, and the doctors found a disease and infection. I wasn't told the details of how bad it was until visiting with a gynecologist specialist the following day. I was shocked when the doctor told me I might need a complete hysterectomy. But after taking eight antibiotics a day, being treated by amazing doctors with great wisdom, and much prayer, I was completely healed. After my surgery the doctor said they couldn't find any sign of disease or infection in me. I received a miracle no one could explain. I wish I could tell you what I went through was a piece of cake, but I can tell you it was worth it.

Going through the heartache of my past marriage and fighting a disease in my body was hard enough, but that wasn't all. I experienced so much emotional pain. People in my life that I thought cared about me chose instead to judge me, throw stones at me, and do whatever they could to crush my heart and spirit. Spreading rumors, false accusations, sharing personal details, and adding their own personal twist seemed to bring them great pleasure. I felt as if the good and positive accomplishments from my life meant nothing anymore. People were so quick with accusations and judgments; they didn't show me any love or grace.

Do you want some words of wisdom? Change your circle of influence and choose people who are positive and filled with encouragement. Invite these people to come closer in your life instead of people who continuously judge you or throw stones at you.

I definitely had bitterness, resentment, anger, unforgiveness, and hatred in my heart that needed to be dealt with. Three years of counseling and the twelve-step spiritual program allowed me to forgive my ex-husband, the family and friends who hurt me, and most of all myself for the poor choices I made. I will be the first to admit I've made some stupid choices in life, but when we learn from our failures, we grow for the better. Now I want others to receive grace, love, and compassion because I know how painful judgment feels.

You may be going through a tough situation right now. You may feel like you're being squeezed from every angle, but you must believe there's a reason. Do not stay home and nurse your problems; fear prevents progress. We have to stop trying to figure everything out and trust that a great plan lies ahead. You have to see spring in the winter. During the winter months, the leaves are off the trees and the scenery looks lifeless and boring. When spring comes, new growth emerges. We have to see the beauty to come (spring) during the long, cold, hard months of our lives (winter).

I encourage you to stand in front of the mirror and state affirmations about yourself. When you come from an abusive relationship and feel like the scum of the earth, it's hard to look in the mirror—I understand. As hard as it was, though, I chose to stand in front of my bathroom mirror daily and read the affirmations I taped to it until I believed what they said: "I am beautiful; I am valued; I have great worth; I am loved; I am unique; I am a change maker; I will make a positive difference in the lives of others."

Seven years after my divorce, I met the man of my dreams. He completely loves and adores me and treats me like a princess. We met while ballroom dancing, and I can literally say that he swept me off my feet. Your time is coming. Whatever you are believing for—a breakthrough in your marriage or with your children, a new job, better health, or more finances—I encourage you to hold on and know there is hope and healing ahead.

Susan Owensby is an author, inspirational speaker, and leader who enjoys sharing her story of hope and healing with women. After an abusive relationship, a difficult divorce, and making plenty of poor choices along the way, her story inspires women to never give up, to fail forward, and to keep going.

www.susanowensby.com

Buoyancy . . . Ballooning
through a Superstorm

Jane Parmel

Nothing is so painful to the human mind as great and sudden change.
Mary Shelley

All week we had been hearing about a coming storm. My partner and I were also gearing up for one of the biggest events we were managing all year. We were busy with orders, design plans, and more; our entire staff was in all week and extremely busy. The local meteorologists were issuing warnings about this hurricane coming up the East Coast—"the storm of the century," "a massive and destructive storm"— and reporting that this storm had all the possibilities of becoming a "superstorm." With each passing day, predictions for landfall and the level of destruction were becoming more dire.

But meteorologists had been wrong in the past, so we crossed our fingers and hoped for the best. The day before our big event, my seventy-nine-year-old mother was rushed to the emergency room. I directed most of the operations in our company, but I dropped everything and spent the day in the ER in Astoria, meeting with doctors and nurses who were trying to determine what my mother was suffering from and how to treat her. My partner and staff handled everything in my absence, but this added to the stress as this was one of the only times I had stepped away at crunch time.

The event went off the next day without a hitch—the party was a success, our clients were thrilled, and everyone had a great time. My lead manager had listened to the weather forecasts and had moved as much equipment as he could up onto tables and workbenches; he secured items that might move; he positioned sandbags at the front door. The store was closed and our staff was safely in their homes on the day of the storm. This was a bad one, and the forecasts were right. "Great and sudden" came in the form of historic Superstorm Sandy.

Coney Island Creek swelled to the north, slowly overflowing its banks and spreading over the neighborhood. We sat home and watched through security cameras as water flooded the streets. A short time later, the storm surge brought the Atlantic Ocean to our doorstep, then through the front door, through the store—five-and-a-half feet of water throughout. The current was swift, coming in and leaving quickly. And the damage? Truly unbelievable.

Equipment, supplies, fixtures, displays, cabinetry—everything was turned upside down, soaked with water, and caked with mud. We had spent twenty years building our business, and now everything was just a pile of garbage. Our tagline was "TFL Party Planners—'Party' Is Our Middle Name." And we indeed planned great parties and events, but the truth was, we never had a plan for destruction on this level, the cleanup, the financing, the staff, the going forward. Not many people do. But we decided to chart our own course, and our resilience came through community.

First, everyone on our staff called to ask, "What's the plan?" They all came in the very next day and started the cleanup. We salvaged what we could and watched the DSNY take away the rest. FEMA offered help, so we began our application process. After so many years of seeing their trucks in other locations throughout our country, it was indeed surreal for me and my partner to now be the ones asking for help. As small business owners, we were so used to doing things ourselves, but now we had to embrace the help that was offered to us. And that help came to us in tremendous ways.

Men we knew from our Coney Island community came by and helped to clean out the entire store; they removed sheetrock and insulation and got us ready to rebuild within the first week. Our network partner, BalloonPlanet.com, headed by Jim Parker, raised funds through a worldwide network of balloon professionals to help us restock our inventory. My partner's brothers made sure our staff had lunch while we cleaned; friends stopped by to see how they could help. Most of our family had similar damage to their homes, and our neighborhood was completely affected. Family friends offered space in their business so we could get back to work.

But one thing stayed ever present for my partner and me, and we've tried our best to pass the concept on. Our resilience came from the fact that we were blessed with another day. Another opportunity to enter a building that others no longer had; a chance to restock, restore, and rebuild. If we had done it once, we could do it again.

We were indeed back to work within the week—with two new scissors from Staples and a new order of inventory. We filled our clients' orders and made deliveries in our own cars. The process with FEMA was long and arduous, and between denials, extensions, and more, a loan was not approved until March 2014. Our return was aided over the years as our misfortune with Sandy led us to greater opportunities: a grant from our local natural gas company, acceptance into Goldman Sachs 10,000 Small Businesses initiative, and workshops and courses given by the NYC Small Business community all helped us to realign our business for a resurgence. We supported our community over the years, and our local and professional communities supported us as well. That support helped us to realize how truly blessed we were—resilient spirits ready to work not because we had to, but because we were able to.

*With over thirty years' experience in education and event management, **Jane Parmel** works to advance coaches, creatives, and small business owners into profitability. She speaks on acceptance, resiliency, and authenticity. As a Global Business Connector for WSA, she connects women with message-advancing resources in a supportive New York community.*

www.janeparmel.com

Step Out of the Shadows and into Your Spotlight

Michela Quilici

All the world's a stage. And all the men and women merely players;
they have their exits and their entrances.
William Shakespeare

Our stage can take many forms, such as a presentation, a conversation with a prospective client, a networking situation, or how we communicate on our website or social media channels. Every day, we are on a stage delivering a message. And each time we make an entrance onto the stage of life, we have an opportunity to inspire, influence, and motivate others.

But most of us don't realize the power we have: the power to influence. Instead, we give our power to influence over to conditioned habits that keep us safe from harm.

Female cultural, societal, and conditioned habits have traditionally revolved around women minimizing their strengths, shrinking back and not taking up space, apologizing, downplaying their accomplishments, and using undermining speech habits.

Brilliant women with important messages and wise insights diminish themselves. They choose to play a supporting role rather than take center stage of their life and business.

I've heard the same stories from business professionals and hundreds of entrepreneurs I've coached. They come to me because they want their voice to be heard and their message to be seen. They want to get clients and grow their business with more confidence and ease.

Here's what I have experienced myself and observed firsthand in my work as the things that hold women back from being seen:

- To be seen means to be vulnerable.
- The voice of the inner critic is the loudest.
- Brilliant women are clever at hiding.
- Fear of failure or success holds us back.

How can we dare to be visible?

Daring to be visible is a leadership quality. It requires the courage to step into your self-leadership.

I believe that for women to be seen and heard, we have to choose to take the stage, and we have to have the courage to stop hiding.

For women with a message who have a deep desire to make a difference in the world, daring to be visible is a requirement. If you want to increase your influence, your income, and your impact, then you must permit yourself to do so.

There are three requirements for being visible:

1. *Lean into Your Vulnerability.* Recognize your hiding strategies for playing small and delaying, and take leaps into playing big right now. Leaping cannot be done in isolation, because taking leaps forces you to confront uncomfortable realities about your vision, and it's too easy to slip into hiding when you're doing it alone. Connect with a community of people who will lovingly call you out when you're hiding and who will call you forward to claim your calling.

2. *Position Your Uniqueness to Be Seen.* Translate the essence of who you are at your core and package it in a way that people see your brilliance. This will magnetize your buyers and compel people to take notice and listen to you. Market leadership and influence are dictated by how well you communicate your distinction and your offering to your audience.

3. *Stand on Your Authority Platform.* Being visible is only the first step. Leaping from being visible to getting known is the key to turning your influence into impact. Standing on a well-known, global platform will give you instant credibility and expert status for opening doors and being the woman to know. Going live on your social channel won't get you there. What I'm talking about is leveraging a truly connected and collaborative platform such as Women Speakers Association.

If you have a deep desire to create real change in the world, now is your time. There are so many people who need your help—right now. If you assume the leadership position, people will gather and follow you.

If you are a coach, entrepreneur, expert, messenger, or business professional, the opportunity you have to support people in these current times is massive. Individuals want to follow a leader. They want to be guided and shown the way forward. If you are a visionary who sees the clearing beyond the storm, then you have a responsibility to lead people through to the other side.

Now is the time that leaders need to step up, gather, and lead communities. We're not going to get through this alone.

The impact you can have when you gather and lead is transformational. Leading empowers people to rise. Gathering in community builds resilience, and by stepping into a leadership role, you can make a difference.

Dare to be visible.

Take the lead.

The world is waiting for you. What are you waiting for?

Michela Quilici is a business navigator, award-winning business growth coach and marketing expert, speaker, and international bestselling author. She is the co-creator of the Global Business Connector Program at WSA and serves on the Forbes Coaches Council. She works with leaders and business owners to help them get noticed, get clients, and get profitable.

www.michelaquilici.com

Pivot, Reframe, Refocus, and Reenergize

Vivien Rayam

Nobody could have imagined that 2020 would be the year of a global pandemic. The rippling effects of COVID-19 are impacting economies globally and may lead to a recession or possibly a depression in the United States. As a result, many small businesses will close by the end of 2020, even with government assistance. As an entrepreneur of a kids' STEM-coding franchise, I've had to grapple with the fear of how to move forward during this unprecedented time. The pandemic hit right when we were about to reach one hundred kids enrolled in our program, after only five months in business—a major milestone.

Interestingly enough, it is during our biggest challenges that we can have our greatest clarity. As the pandemic numbers increased, we shuttered our doors and tried virtual programming for a short time, then opted to provide free programming to our customers and freeze all payments until we reopened. Now, this may not be a popular strategy. However, having two months to design our reopening plan was exactly what we needed. The keys to our business resiliency strategy is fourfold: *Pivot, Reframe, Refocus,* and *Reenergize.*

The great thing about having a business resiliency strategy is that you have a plan in place to help you navigate the uncertainty of the market. The *Pivot* approach focuses on the need to assess how your business has to change as a result of the new circumstance. I determined that we would need options virtually and in-person, and for the kids that were in our center, safety was key. We also had to cut expenses, so we moved from a six-days-a-week operation to four days. Monthly budgets were readjusted, and we applied for all government funding that was applicable for our business. Lastly, we contacted lenders and vendors to see how we could lower our expenses. All of these steps allowed us to cut our expenses by 35 percent. Learning to pivot places you in the right frame of mind to adapt to the unexpected situation and look for the opportunity hidden in the challenge.

In the midst of a pandemic when everything seems grim, the need to *Reframe* is critical. The act of reframing forces you to look at the current situation with a new lens. At times like this, if you were conducting a SWOT analysis on your business, you should only be focusing on the opportunities. Some questions to ask yourself include: *Are there new customers I can reach? Are there new strategic partnerships I need to build? What new programs do I need, or how do I adjust the current ones for the current climate?*

As I looked at my business, I knew that kids who were usually in sports would be available now. Other kids would need a break from digital learning, so coming into the center could be an option for those families. Additionally, partnering with schools to provide virtual programming would help fill the void lost from no after-school programs. It also became clear that there was a need for more virtual programming, so we looked at ways to adjust our offering to provide in-person and virtual options. There were many other questions I asked myself, but the questions noted earlier put me on the path to reframe the situation to see the possibilities in the business.

Recharged after using the reframing approach, I was able to *Refocus* on what the business is today with the new opportunities. The ability to refocus allows twenty-twenty vision for the road ahead as you consider both the opportunities and the potential threats. Nobody wants to talk about the worst-case scenarios, but if you don't, you can't determine plans to circumvent the situation. It is basically looking your fear in the eye and saying, "Not today, not ever—I've worked too hard and come too far to fail." I looked at various enrollment amounts and what we would need to stay afloat. I looked at scenarios that took into account the length of time before things returned to the new normal. At the end of the day, I had to make a decision to stay the course through the pandemic, however long it would take, and I had to trust that the business would be stronger as a result.

Once I was clear on our direction, I just needed to *Reenergize* myself for the race ahead. It is nonstop, ever-changing, exhausting, and as I've discovered, it's the most fulfilling race you will ever run. This act of bringing back your energy is vital because you will need it for the ups and downs that will come. I also had to energize staff, students, parents, and the community at large about our services and what we have to offer.

If I could shout it from the rooftops, I would: GET A BUSINESS RESILENCY PLAN! Aside from the coding business, I also serve as a business coach for new and emerging women entrepreneurs, helping them create a roadmap for success and build a sustainable business in line with their gifts and purpose. I would love to tell you that the *Pivot, Reframe, Refocus, Reenergize* business resiliency strategy is the number-one plan for business success to navigate through a pandemic. I can't—because I am still in the thick of it myself. But without my business resiliency plan, I might have already closed my doors.

As an entrepreneur, you have to be ready for unexpected change and learn to be flexible, develop new processes, cut expenses, and adapt as situations arise. The *Pivot, Reframe, Refocus, Reenergize* business resiliency strategy allows for quick action, strategic thinking, assessing opportunities while noting risks, and ensuring you have the energy and right frame of mind to move ahead with a clear direction and a plan in hand.

Vivien Rayam is a business coach for purpose-driven women entrepreneurs and an international bestselling author. As general manager and co-owner of Code Ninjas Snellville in Georgia, she works with youth to help them develop a love of computer programming and foster an interest in STEM careers.

www.vivienrayam.com

POST NUBILA PHOEBUS (AFTER THE CLOUDS, SUN)

Samantha A. Roman

We all have a great many stories. The easy ones to share are those of triumph; the captivating ones recognize vulnerabilities and overcoming obstacles along the way. All teach us lessons we can either heed or ignore at our own peril.

It was an early spring morning following a particularly gray winter, the kind that leaves the body anemic for the sun's glow and warmth. Through the opened window an uncomfortably frosty breeze felt poetically appropriate to mark the ending of a once-promising business relationship. The betrayal I felt came from knowing that my funding of cannabinoid-based health projects for women and veterans would need to be delayed. As an advisor, it was difficult to witness the "leadership" team I had been working with turn against one another at such an early stage. Unfettered greed and infighting had all but halted building the core business and shifted the focus to scheming and litigation. Details aside, when a business starts compromising its integrity specifically and its values generally, it signals that even good people are losing their way.

Now wise to the unfortunate truth, it was time for me to leave. I glanced one last time at the computer screen before hitting send to end the relationship. This was not an easy decision; it would require significant effort to find another team, this time with the right combination of talent and values. The swooshing sound of the electronic mail disappearing into the ether of cyberspace was followed by a silence that was neither final nor fulfilling—but it was right.

As it turns out, experience is a rather ruthless teacher. I spent the next couple of weeks alone, thinking and learning. In silence I evaluated events of the past year and refined my approaches to advisory work. Incorporating notes from experiences I'd had with nearly one hundred companies resulted in the creation of two books full of lessons. The first book focuses on the complexity of leading successful, sustainable organizations while managing risk. The second, an evolution of personal lessons, observations, and shared wisdom including the following advice.

You are your own best friend. The only factor that you can effectively control is yourself. When you are alone and most vulnerable, the one person that will be there for the rest of your life is you. It's easy to overlook this fact. To set a long-term course requires deep and honest introspection to understand what is most important to you, and why. Make sure you reflect on what really inspires you enough that you are willing to go it alone if required. Don't avoid asking the tough questions; doing so helps you choose values and come to terms with the consequence of the actions needed to uphold and defend them.

To go far, you need others. There is tremendous comfort to be gained in seeking the advice from beloved friends, family, and admired mentors. Second and third opinions not only test the clarity of your thinking and validate when you are aligned with others, but they also identify blind spots. Paradoxically, those who nurture relationships become more independent just by knowing there is a social safety net should they stumble. Similarly, contributing to the development and enrichment of others can also transform your perspective about personal setbacks, and this will lead to collaborative growth opportunities. In short, building a collaborative support network is foundational.

Finally, choose a positive attitude. The stories you tell yourself are incredibly important, whether they are true or not. As in nature, after the clouds there is always sun, so staying focused on long-term outcomes is a powerful way to focus your efforts, especially in times of conflict and uncertainty. Although it seems easier said than done, telling yourself "Whatever you may be experiencing is not the worst possible case" supports a grateful mindset. When you embrace the idea that there is always something to be thankful for, attention is drawn to looking forward to the good things in life, however small. When you are positive, you demonstrate self-confidence and the ability to respond to whatever comes your way. Being positive can change your life.

Four months later, after considerable self-reflection, I started advising a more effective executive team. Clear-eyed stock-taking and the unwavering support of my network had provided the structural elements needed to recover. Together, we had made it through the eye of the storm. Through experience I had reaffirmed how powerful confidence and a sense of self are to springboard growth.

At the best of times, it takes courage to share challenging personal experiences. It can be daunting to lower our defenses and reveal missteps, which may be judged harshly by some. With this in mind, know that however long and lonely a path seems, the courage to maintain the strength of our convictions binds those who are willing to go the distance. And in the toughest of times, when plagued by loss or disappointment, inspiration from others comes in many forms if you are willing to listen. In the words of Alfred, Lord Tennyson:

> *Tho' much is taken, much abides; and though*
> *We are not now that strength which in old days*
> *Moved earth and heaven; that which we are, we are;*
> *One equal temper of heroic hearts,*
> *Made weak by time and fate, but strong in will*
> *To strive, to seek, to find, and not to yield.*

Be bold, do good, and pursue what you love.

Samantha A. Roman is an entrepreneur and CEO of the advisory Credible Cannabis. Since selling her first company to Canopy Growth Corporation, she has become a trusted media figure recognized for her insights, business integrity, and grit. She holds a Bachelor of Science (Nursing) and a Master of Business Administration.

www.samantharoman.com

A LIFETIME WORTH SPENDING

DeLisa Rose

LIFE is a four-letter word that is complicated enough that no one can ever say with certainty what life is really all about. Yet everyone wants to get it right; hence, everyone is spending precious time day in, day out trying to live their best lives while pursuing what it ideally means to be alive.

Like so many others, I found myself spending my time going through the monotony of a life driven and determined to achieve success, yet ignorant and oblivious to what success really is.

Allow me to introduce myself. I am a nationally accomplished real estate broker. I've been recognized in the top 1 percent of Realtors in the country. I've been the recipient of three Hall of Fame awards and honored by the National Association of Realtors as one of the Most Inspiring Realtors. My Community Partner of the Year Award for my community service and philanthropic work is one of my favorite honors; it tops my personal meetings and experiences with Oprah. After more than twenty years of helping people like yourself buy, sell, and invest in real estate, the awards and titles that scream SUCCESSFUL DIVA AND BOSS BABE can sound pretty impressive. Well . . . *outward perception is not necessarily inner reality.*

I was born and raised in Oakland, California, one of the most poverty-stricken inner cities in the United States. I learned how to cook drugs when I was in elementary school, and by the time I was in high school, I'd been shot at three too many times. I'm willing to bet that hell on earth was the Bay Area during my youth. I'm still in disbelief that after everything I endured, including being a teenage mom, I managed to walk across the UC Berkeley graduation platform while holding the hand of my six-year-old daughter, J'Lynn. *Resilience is everything.*

Although afraid, I mustered up the courage gained from my graduation victory to leap away from a toxic environment. Although I didn't know what the new environment had in store for me, I realized that change requires change and nothing would ever change if I didn't change!

Searching for the "real world and life," I entered into real estate. I aspired to eliminate poverty and build communities. In my first four months in real estate, I earned $119,000. I began earning mid-six figures in my mid-twenties. I bought my little mansion, owned five luxury cars, and hired a nanny. I had ARRIVED—and I was absolutely miserable. I was working endlessly. I had lots of *nice things* that people strive for, yet I was continuously spending the majority of my time on a mission to get bigger, better, smarter, wiser, thinner, and more valuable. I had so much and so little. *Money buys materials, not matters of fulfillment.* I had no time, no peace, and no internal happiness. I was absent of life.

One day when I was on the mountaintop of my so called "success," I received a call. "Everyone has been trying to reach you," they said. "Your voicemail is full, and you haven't answered your calls."

"My bad," I said. "I've been busy, focused on work, and I haven't had much time for small talk." I quickly added, "I'm swamped, and I have to go into a meeting—what's up?"

"Ah, Delisa, you don't know yet, do you?" They now wished that they, too, had been unable to reach me, as they went on to tell me that my sister and her family had been in a major four-car accident on Easter Sunday. Seven people were injured, and five died, including my sister (age thirty-seven), brother, niece (age nine), and nephew (two months).

I remember having an out-of-body experience. Before being able to fully grieve those deaths, more news arrived that one of my grandparents had died, followed by my mom being admitted into ICU.

Shortly after all this trauma, my lupus flared like fireworks, and I found myself completely unable to move the right half of my body. As I waited for the paramedics to arrive, I immediately thought about my children, my family, and my imaginary God (who *is* real). I wanted to make more memories with them; I wanted to feel their kisses and their love. I wanted to hear their laughter. I searched through my memory bank, reviewing the forty years of my life. *Did I tell them everything I wanted to? Was my estate plan ironclad? Does my family know how much I love them? Do they have enough positive memories to last throughout their lifetime?*

Sadly, I didn't have enough memories that I liked. I ran out of personal memories before the ambulance arrived. I wanted to give my family more, tell them more; I wanted to LIVE more. The home, the cars, the life insurance would all be nice for them to have. Yet the whole point of earning monetary success had been to enjoy it with them. Did I achieve success in acquiring things, yet fail at the end goal and measure of success with the way I spent time living life? Fortunately I recovered; the paralysis was temporary. But the entire season was a true wake-up call for me.

I see far too many people burning the engine that manages our health and sanity, calling it being driven for success! I think about my loved ones who are gone. Each life had a different story. And life and work go on without them. It doesn't matter how much time we spend on the earth or how much money we've made and splurged. It doesn't matter how many people like or don't like us. What matters is how we spend each moment that makes up our lifetime. Most people spend their lives working and fail at enjoying the life they live while they work. Make sure your time is better spent than money.

I realize now that I work to live, not live to work. I hope you really experience the small moments, thoughts, and conversations that make up your precious lifetime. If you knew you would die tomorrow, how would you spend your time living today? That is what I hope you spend more time doing.

DeLisa Rose is a Real Estate Broker, author, speaker, podcaster (Dee Rose For Real), coach, mother, and wife. A Hall of Fame and Lifetime Achievement recipient, she educates and inspires others to build financial, mental, emotional, and physical wealth so they can spend time living a lifetime that matters FOR REAL.

www.delisarose.com

MUSINGS OF A COVID-19 BABY

Anita D. Russell

Technologized. Dehumanized. Devalued.
Societal bias favors outward appearance over inward heart.
Cultural conformity is a form of hypocrisy.
Alas, Jesus did not fit the form of a king.
As someone asked, "What good can come from Nazareth?"

I was born on March 14, 2020, the grandson of Anita D. Russell. I am a melanized baby boy born into a world plagued simultaneously by two viruses—one biological, one systemic. Both have the potential to end my life prematurely, to cause me irreparable harm, or to otherwise kill my dreams and aspirations. Poet laureate Langston Hughes, in his poem "Harlem," prophetically asks the question, "What happens to a dream deferred?" In another poem called "Dreams," Mr. Hughes instructs us to hold on to our dreams because if they die, our life becomes like a broken-winged bird or like a barren field frozen with snow.

I was born into a world that has been technologized, dehumanized, and filled with social bias that calls for conformity and sameness. My grandmother—I call her Gam—recently read an article that said CEOs generally fit certain characteristics: tall, deep voice, physically fit, male, white. These are the things that epitomize society's perception of the ideal American CEO—basically a white alpha male. Alpha males are defined as those at the top of the social hierarchy with access to money and power, accumulated through physical prowess, intimidation, and domination. These are the same characteristics in people that have the potential to defer, break, or otherwise freeze my dreams and aspirations.

I was born into a world where some look at me—even when I giggle and coo as babies do—and see nothing more than a future criminal, prisoner, drug addict (or dealer); someone who was born into a life destined for the bottom rung of a social ladder or the bottom of a jelly-bean bag; someone who cannot possibly have a dream, aspiration, or desire to do much good in the world. The school-to-prison pipeline. Mass incarceration. Racism, hatred, violence, and fear. Fear is in the air, and tension is everywhere. Why? Because of the color of my skin. The Temptations were right when they called the world a ball of confusion.

I was born into a world where others look at me—even when I poop and pee as babies do—and see someone who should be free to decide for themselves how they want to live and be, as long as they do it separately. As long as they don't believe they can live in a gated community with the right to make it home after buying Skittles. As long as they don't believe they can live in a community with the right to make it home after a jog. Or as long as they don't believe they can be in their own home, in the middle of the night, playing video games with their nephew, with the right to see the sun rise. After all, law and order must be preserved at all costs.

I was born into a resilient family where they all look at me—even when I struggle to crawl and walk as babies do—and see so much more in me than meets the worldly eye. They see a future father, husband, creative, college grad, entrepreneur; someone who is young, gifted, and black; someone with dreams and aspirations that could transform the world. They believe I can fly like a bird in the sky, soar to the sun, look down at the sea, and know what it means to be free, like Nina. (Hey, my mom's middle name is Simone with a "y.") These are the people who love me, teach me, and believe in me, knowing I was created by God according to his plan, not the plan of man. These are the people who know I was born into this world with immeasurable gifts, a treasure trove of talents, and a purpose to be fulfilled. Jeremiah 29:11 says that God knows the plans he has for me; plans to prosper me and not harm me; plans to give me hope and a future.

I was born into an amazing family. Gam has a master's degree in education. She is a life coach, speaker, and three-time bestselling author. She is a social entrepreneur, a change cultivator who inspires women to be seen and heard. My mom is a Howard University graduate who danced across the country with Princess Jasmine and Aladdin. My dad works independently in the insurance industry. My auntie is a VIP account manager for a gaming company. My big cousin is a junior high school student, a baseball player, and a skateboarder. These are the people with whom I have lived in the house since I was born.

(I was born at the beginning of masks and quarantine.) They keep me safe, clean, and healthy. They protect me from all the forces out there that have the potential (or the desire) to wreak havoc in my life.

I was born into a line of protesters. My great-grandma was an activist who protested. Gam protested. My mom and auntie protested after the killing of George Floyd. As she, auntie, and a different big cousin prepared to go out, my mom asked Gam if she thought I would have to protest in my lifetime. At the time I was three months old. My protesting would make four generations of protesting for the same thing: the right to exist peacefully as a human being in melanized skin.

Now, which person do you see in yourself?
The one who sees me as a future criminal?
The one who sees me with limited rights?
Or a protector of the future of thousands of babies just like me,
born into a society infected with the virus of injustice and inequity?
I am the dream of the former enslaved,
representing the future of freedom so yearned for.
To protect yourself, you must protect me.

Anita D. Russell loves doing BIG things—building community, inspiring women, and giving back. She founded The Place to SOAR to cultivate change that unleashes human potential. I Wanna See Laney's House is her autobiographical narrative. She is the Global Business Connector for Women Speakers Association in Pittsburgh, Pennsylvania.

www.iwannaseelaneyshouse.com

Excuse Me, Your Personality Is Showing

Janet J. Sawyer, EdD

The best thing to hold on to in life is each other.
Audrey Hepburn

The COVID-19 epidemic was a shock to the whole world in 2020. We all had to stay home, and our lives changed forever. Many of us found ourselves spending more time with our spouses and children, while some of us found ourselves alone. We got busy cleaning, cooking, doing puzzles, and connecting with our families by computer or the phone. Well, I was one of those people that found myself alone. You see, all of my family lives in other cities and states.

One of the things I did in order to stay connected to my family members was to be involved in a family Zoom meeting every Sunday afternoon at 1:00 p.m. Pacific Time. During these meetings, we all shared what was going on in our lives. When it was my turn, I shared the work I was doing, which was leadership coaching virtually. But instead of talking about what I was coaching, I invited my family to do an activity I do with my clients. I introduced them to the four DISC personality styles.

So, what is DISC, you might ask? DISC is a language to describe behavior that was first invented by William Moulton-Marston in 1928. Back then he studied people in insane asylums. However, he was very interested in also studying the observable behaviors of normal people. William wrote a book called *Emotions of Normal People*, which is still read today. He was also involved in the early women's rights movement. He had a commitment to the feminist movement that appeared in the form of "comic books" with a female heroine called Wonder Woman. Isn't that great!

Well, to my surprise, my family all agreed to do the activity, and each family member took the DISC assessment. DISC is an acronym that stands for four different personality styles: Dominance, Influence, Steadiness, and Compliance. On one of our calls we tried to guess what each person's style was, and then we shared our results. We learned so much more about one another, and it gave us a better understanding of ourselves, each family member, and how we relate to our friends.

"I learned why my communication style offends some people and connects with others. No wonder some people think I'm a B***H at times!" My niece Arlett said. She is one of the High Ds in the family. Ds are fast-paced and like to focus on tasks to get results. We learned that when we are talking with Arlett, we need to give her the facts and not a lot of details. One of her Character Virtue Strengths is Assertiveness.

Kelli, another niece, is the High I of the family. She has many balls in the air all at once. I'm not sure how she does it, but it's exciting to watch. An I is fast-paced and likes to focus on people. Kelli is full of ideas, so she is the perfect person to brainstorm ideas with. One of her Character Virtue Strengths is Trust.

Zan, my sister-in-law, said, "Now is the perfect time to think about who we are and how we interact with those we love and care about." This is so like Zan because she steadies the pace for our family. Zan is our perfect High S. An S is slow-paced, and they also like to focus on people. One of Zan's Character Virtue Strengths is Patience.

My twin brother, Jimmy, is our High C. He said, "I would have liked more details about the assessment." Cs are slow-paced and focus on details. Jimmy loves to know how and why things work. One of his Character Virtue Strengths is Integrity.

And what is my style? Well, I have something in common with my niece Arlett. I am a High D too!

To summarize, as a family we learned that if you are speaking to a "Bottom-Line Results Person" or a "High D" (Dominance-style Arlett and me), you need to be direct and get to the point. If you are a talkative "People-Person," you are what we call a "High I" (Influence-style Kelli). If you are interacting with a "High S" (Steadiness-style Zan), you will want to be calm, easygoing, and patient. And with a "High C" (Compliance-style Jimmy), make sure you are organized and prepared when speaking to them. Doing this activity with my family has made us feel more connected than ever!

What Is Your Primary DISC Style?

These four very different DISC styles have very different needs, emotions, and fears. Learning and understanding your DISC personality style helps you build rapport, appreciate the differences in others, and positively influence those around you.

Do you remember the Golden Rule: "Do unto others as you would have them do unto you"? The PeopleSmart World founders, Sandra Davis and Carol Dysart, believe in the Platinum Rule, which states that when you understand your DISC style(s), you will "adapt, and treat people the way they like to be treated, NOT the way you like to be treated." With this understanding, you will be able to develop the type of relationships you really want!

You might be thinking, *How do I find out my DISC Style?* Great question! Do you have ten to fifteen minutes to find out? If the answer is yes, I would like to invite you to go to jjsawyerconsulting.com and take your free DISC assessment. When you click submit, you will receive your results. When reading your results, make sure you click on the ten-minute video link. This video will help you better understand the styles.

As you're getting closer to your family members, friends, clients and co-workers virtually, my wish for you is to try this activity and discover different personalities unfolding before your eyes! I guarantee the conversations will be priceless!

Janet J. Sawyer, EdD, is the CEO and founder of JJ Sawyer Consulting, LLC. She is a leadership development coach, certified in the PeopleSmart DISC Interpretation Method and an international bestselling author. She specializes in coaching her clients on how to apply leadership strategies when working with others. Dr. Sawyer currently lives in Carlsbad, California.

www.jjsawyerconsulting.com

Be Positive, Pursue Your Dreams, and Never Quit

Linda Payton Thompson

A positive mindset and a positive attitude bring about positive thinking and positive speaking. Our words are powerful and daily create our lives. During these uncertain times, it is imperative for us to remain positive and expect the best, even when we are forced to experience isolation from our families and the daily routine of everyday living is disrupted.

Who imagined that we would be living in a time when, due to COVID-19, we would be quarantined and isolated from our families and friends? Who could have imagined that we'd be forced to work from home (or be furloughed), become teachers due to schools shutting down, be restricted from going to the gym, restaurants, churches, movies, and beaches? None of us saw it coming; none of us were ready for the effects the pandemic has had on us or the rearranging and adjustment that would need to be made.

Well, I certainly wasn't prepared mentally or emotionally because I am a person who loves networking and being with family and friends. Prior to COVID-19, I was out of the house at least three to four days a week volunteering and going to the gym, and I always looked forward to line dancing. I was doing live speaking events just like everyone else, and then that came to a halt.

In March when social distancing and all the recommendations were put in place, I was okay with it because I knew it was supposed to be for the best, only last a short while, and then things would return to normal. But when four months had passed, it was clear that there would no getting back to normal anytime soon, and social distancing would still be mandatory. That's when I started feeling really isolated. I had just retired from public health case management social work after twenty-seven years of working with moms in the maternity clinic, which I had thoroughly enjoyed. I had planned to get the message out about my two books, do speaking engagements, coach and consult, travel, visit family, and enjoy life. Social distancing put a halt to all that.

One good thing about this time of COVID-19 was that I had to pivot and readjust to new ways of doing things online. At first, I was productive with my various projects, and I was getting used to being online more. But I missed the weekly human contact of being with my fitness buddies, seeing family members, being with my church family, traveling out of town to sightsee, planning getaways to the resorts, and going shopping. I missed hugs because I am a hugger. All of this began to affect me emotionally.

One of my sisters had to be admitted to a nursing home for rehab, and two days later her daughter passed. My niece Angel and her husband had a baby boy, which made me happy, but the next day I found out that my cousin Sam, who I was very close to, passed. All of this happened in one week.

The worst part was that I couldn't go visit any of my relatives due to social distancing. I couldn't attend the funerals or visit my sister or my niece. This was very hard on me because I've always tried to be there for support when something happens. Finally, in June, I decided I had to shake this somehow.

I experienced a wakeup call when my friend Betty called and asked me how I was doing. I was laying on the couch watching TV when she called, and I said, "I'm okay," but in my heart I knew I wasn't. We talked for a minute or two and then hung up. After the call I told my husband, Eddie, that I was not okay. I called Betty back an hour later after I had a good cry, and I told her that I had to somehow get away for a while because I was missing my family and right now, I was not OK. Betty told me, "I knew it, because you always encourage me, and I felt something was different."

I told Betty that I realized that I had to acknowledge my feelings and make a decision to do something. I told her that my plan was to leave town and visit my son and his family again and start taking short road trips at least twice a week just to sightsee. I planned to cut down on the amount of news I was watching. I would start exercising online, and I would continue to watch my church services online in order to keep my connection. I also decided I would only watch inspiring or funny movies, and I would begin reaching out to family and friends on a particular day of the week. Most of all, I would accept the time that we are in now, continue to pursue all my projects, and not give up.

I did leave town to refresh, reinvent, and press forward. I had written two books, and I knew that sharing my message with the world was important. I readjusted my focus, and I chose to persevere.

To everyone reading this, my message is simple. Don't quit, acknowledge where you are, and make any necessary adjustments. You can speak positive words over your situation and expect the victory. Be encouraged! Stay positive! Be resilient!

Linda Payton Thompson empowers, inspires, and encourages individuals to live their best life possible by removing challenges and roadblocks that hinder. She encourages women to believe in themselves, knowing without a doubt that they are beautiful and valuable. Linda is an author, speaker, and certified health and life coach.

www.lindathompsonspeaker.com

FIND HEALING THROUGH ART

Cate Tuitt, MBE

Creativity and your unique artistic expression give you a voice. You do not have to be a Van Gogh! Creativity is a way to heal physically, mentally, and spiritually, an avenue to arise from the global lockdown, and the key to open out into your world. To express yourself when you struggle to find the words, or when you are angry, despairing, or confused.

I personally recommend it; I found it immensely useful after I was discharged from the hospital after a serious illness a few years ago. I had been advised to stay at home to recuperate, and during that time I began to draw and paint. Whenever my visitors asked me what they could bring me, or asked me if I needed any chocolates, I would ask for paint and papers.

I can honestly say it healed me faster than if I had just watched TV. It was so liberating, and I was able to explore the feelings I experienced during my recovery on paper and through my drawings and paintings.

Everyone has a creative side. You may have found yours blocked by the recent COVID-19 pandemic. Or you may not have discovered yours yet. The ideas in this chapter can help you to calm your mind and body through the difficult times in your life. These ideas might spark a way to bring you the delight, excitement, joy, happiness, and peace you deserve.

On this journey through life, you will experience a lot of twists and turns. These defining moments will lead you to your true self—your life's purpose. It is often through the gift of pain, struggles, and chaos that we stumble on our calling. Our circumstances are the gifts that give us the resolve to keep on giving. They help us awaken to our essence, our true being of self-expression.

Art therapy can help you to resolve conflicts, develop social skills, reduce stress, and increase self-esteem. Here are some of the advantages and benefits that art therapy provides:

Expressing feelings that are difficult to verbalize—Sometimes it is difficult for us to express what we feel or what we think, which is why art therapy, a tool that uses and develops expression, can help you to give shape to these thoughts.

Exploring imagination and creativity—When using this type of self-therapy, you will explore your true capacity to be able to create and imagine.

Developing healthy coping skills—Facing your feelings and emotions in a creative way can help you to change established behaviors and habits that no longer serve you and face difficult situations in a healthy way.

Identifying and clarifying of issues and concerns—Expressing in the external world that which concerns us internally makes us see in a more practical and accessible way those concepts we cannot understand.

Improved self-esteem and confidence—The process of personal growth allows us to listen and understand ourselves, thus offering ourselves a positive valuation and favorable self-concept. By doing the work for ourselves, we can achieve a better emotional stability and achieve our goals.

Increased communication capacity—By using the artistic model to express ourselves, we acquire new tools to have good communication with one another as well as with ourselves. Performing personal and therapeutic work in a safe environment allows us to express ourselves better emotionally and rediscover ourselves.

Improved motor skills and physical coordination—Art therapy normally uses the body to express what we cannot say, so this type of healing also assists those people who have difficulty when making or coordinating movements.

Decreased stress and anxiety—Carrying out activities related to art and creativity give you an experience in which both your stress and anxiety levels are reduced.

Healing art therapy is highly effective when you are dealing with difficult life processes. Below are some of the occurrences of life where art therapy is most often indicated as therapy. These benefits can be obtained by anyone.

- Transitions of life
- Global pandemics, such as COVID-19
- Experiences of pain, loss, and grief
- Learning and self-care
- Controlling stress and anxiety levels
- Addressing unresolved conflicts
- Dealing with depression
- Difficulties in emotional expression
- Traumatic experiences such as natural disasters and accidents
- Blocked feelings and hopelessness
- Emotional processing of a non-favorable medical diagnosis
- Feelings of isolation or loneliness
- Fear and anxiety at the idea of death
- Substance abuse and eating disorders
- Conflicts related to the concept of identity

You do not need to have some type of disorder or mental problem to enjoy this type of psychotherapy. The benefits can be applied to anyone. My paintings drew me out of my pain and enabled me to express my hopes and fears without struggling to find the words.

Once I was back to work, I introduced the techniques to my clients, and they have provided feedback on how healing through art has assisted them with everything from depression to domestic violence. No matter what your situation might be, art therapy can provide healing and restore well-being.

Cate Tuitt, MBE, is a motivational speaker, trainer, and consultant. She studied law at university in London and worked for over twenty-five years in justice and law organizations. Her experience with clients who had negative experiences motivated Cate to explore the power of art to assist others to overcome trauma and rebuild their lives.

www.catetuittbooks.com

Become an Unstoppable Thinker and Reclaim Your Future

Cheryl Verrett

Nothing can stop one who is determined to succeed.
Author Unknown

Today more than ever, I believe that our voices are necessary to be the change the world needs. The time is now to have an unwavering determination to emerge and go from stuck to unstoppable! It's time to step out of your comfort zone, take risks, and dream again. Allow your life to display resiliency, strength, and courage. People are waiting for you to reveal possibilities!

I understand how easy it is to want to give up when life hurts. In one season of my life, I went from having everything to having nothing. You see, in the early 2000s the real estate industry crashed, forcing me to close my doors and leaving me only with broken dreams and hope deferred. I was devastated. A tornado of emotions in an unexplored valley of despair, heartbreak, frustration, and feelings of embarrassment seemed to have me spinning. For a moment, I felt stuck because instead of planning my future, I was strategically planning how to transition from owning everything to owning nothing. My life and my identity were disrupted. I questioned my value and impact in the world.

As my family and I sat outside one evening looking at the stars, my children asked, "Where do we go from here? Are we quitting?" As I turned to them and saw their eyes quizzically looking for an answer, something stirred inside of me, and it was if I was jolted back to reality. I reflected on the other times I had experienced setbacks only to bounce back. *If I did it then, I can do it again*, I thought. Some of my greatest victories and biggest breakthroughs in life arose from the greatest pains and the hardest challenges I had experienced.

There is a quote by Les Brown that says, "The graveyard is the richest place on earth, because it's here that you'll find all the hopes and dreams that were never fulfilled, the books that were never written, the songs that were never sung, the inventions that were never shared, the cures that were never discovered, all because someone was too afraid to take that first step, keep with the problem, or determined to carry out their dream." I was determined to emerge and become unstoppable, to be the example of what is possible.

When I take my last breath, I want it to be said that "Cheryl lived a life poured out. She birthed her dreams, wrote her books, and sang her songs." I needed to teach my children how to stand against the adversities of life and keep pushing and striving for their dreams. I needed them to see the other side of defeat. I had to emerge from an emotional state that was not serving my future.

What I have come to learn and believe is that in those challenging moments, we must fight the thoughts in our mind like our life depends upon it, because it does. Life is 10 percent what we do and 90 percent what we think. The things we focus on the most grow and manifest in our lives. The mind is the key to winning or losing the battle! I had to transform my mindset and become an Unstoppable Thinker.

Unstoppable Thinkers visualize, focus, and then execute. To go places you've never gone, you have to do things you've never done. The plan and purpose for my life had not changed, but I created a new blueprint. I revisualized my future with me prospering and walking in new possibilities. I specifically detailed goals, action steps, and deadlines. I was driven by my desire to create something new. I was driven by my desire to leave a legacy of the unstoppable mentality for my children.

Unstoppable Thinkers know that what you focus on the most and give your attention to grows. Therefore, I couldn't allow the negative emotions to take root by focusing on what I lost, but instead I had to focus on the wins, impact, and value given. Eleanor Roosevelt stated, "All of the water in the world can't drown you unless it gets inside of you." Therefore, I focused on reading books and listening to tapes that encouraged me to grow and stay in action. I surrounded myself with people who had experienced great loss but were now high achievers. I enlisted coaches, some of whom I never met that coached me from afar. I knew that if I continued to plant good seeds, one day I would have a good harvest. I stayed in action. As I stayed in action, I gained momentum. As I gained momentum, the negative emotions swirling in my head dissipated as I filled my mind with valuable information, leaving no room for anything else.

Unstoppable Thinkers execute plans by staying in action, focusing on the solution, not the problem. When the market crashed, I was devastated, but I used my frustrations and disappointments as fuel to get into action. To this day, Verrett 4 Homes Real Estate company is alive and thriving because I did not give up. My children are entrepreneurs because together we stayed in action.

Even though I would not wish anyone to experience a great loss, I am now stronger and more courageous because I did. After losing everything, I began to use my voice as a motivational speaker and coach to equip others to turn crisis into opportunities, to stay in action, and to reclaim their future. The greatest adventure I ever experienced was my most challenging. Through it all, the verse "'For I know the plans I have for you,' declares the Lord, 'plans to prosper you and not to harm you, plans to give you hope and a future'" (Jeremiah 29:11) gave me the encouragement necessary to focus, execute a plan, and stay in action—which then allowed me to emerge, go from stuck to unstoppable, and reclaim my future!

*The co-owner of a real estate company, **Cheryl Verrett** is also a speaker, author, and coach. Cheryl assists women to shatter self-doubt, release untapped potential, and experience personal and professional growth. She coaches her clients to stay in action, gain momentum, accelerate their vision, and become unstoppable.*

www.cherylverrett.com

THE ANSWER IS TO BE!

Karen J. Watson

I wait for the surgeon to crack open my breastbone to break my heart and save me.

Twenty-seven years before, when I was thirty-three, my new family doctor listened to my heart with concern. She sent me to a cardiologist, who explained that I have a congenital heart defect: a bicuspid aortic valve. Once I develop symptoms, without surgery I'll be dead within two years. The serious symptoms include extreme shortness of breath, fainting, and heart pain. They could happen at any time. The whole mortality thing just got real.

I make changes. I practice calming the mind, doing yoga, tai chi, and meditation, and I strengthen my heart and body muscles with weights and cardio. I love well and make two wonderful babies with my Italian husband at the time. I write and draw when I can. I prepare a will. I work hard and feel tired and stressed. I worry that my children will grow up without a mother, so I treasure each moment. We spend hours on park swings and swimming in the lake. We talk about dreams, good and bad. We smell lots of roses. We laugh at silly jokes as their father learns English and they forget Italian.

I live with uncertainty. And one day I faint as I dash to my car. It's time. The heart surgery is scheduled. I plan for the worst . . . hope for the best. I say goodbye to friends and family. I place my fate into the hands of the crackerjack team at the University of Ottawa Heart Institute.

They knock me out and put me on a heart-lung machine that pumps and breathes for me. The surgeon saws through my breastbone, cuts open my heart, and slices out the calcified aortic valve. He sews in a cow valve, twist-ties my bone together, and delicately sews up my chest skin. He tells my partner I've been a model patient. He's amazed I had such quality of life—my valve was so blocked and brittle, a piece could have broken off and sliced my arteries at any time.

I wake up in the ICU. "How do you feel?" they ask me.

"Dazed," I say—not a medical term but exactly how I feel. They move me to a room beside a very ill patient. I am wired to monitors; I'm in pain and deeply bruised from the blood thinner I was given.

On Day Three, I code—I almost die from heart block. Alarms ring all over the Heart Institute as I fall backwards down a long, dark tunnel. I'm calm as I drift away . . . and then they save my life a second time. Meanwhile a doctor pulls my partner aside and asks about a "do not resuscitate" order in case I'm stuck in that dark tunnel. As I come to, the room is full of concerned faces asking if I know where I am.

On Day Four, I'm not okay. I get transfusions, more drugs. I feel odd and stunned. They poke me. I am compliant. I obey.

I have raging nightmares night after night, waking up drenched in sweat. I hurt all over. My senses are hyper-alert. I'm scared of the new drugs and my sensitivity to them. It hurts when I cough. But I breathe deeply as instructed. I obey.

On Day Five, I stabilize. I feel like myself again and outpace expectations. There is pure joy when I see my family and friends. At night doors still slam, and I only sleep for an hour at a time. Nurses run in and out at my neighbor's distress signals and beeping medication pumps. Lights flip on; doors bang open. Voices rise and fall.

My instinct is to stay sane. The doctor says I can leave the hospital the next day if I'm ready. My family and friends freak out. "She was totally unstable a day ago—this is only Day Five!"

My partner has been strong, but now he is falling apart. It's too soon, he says. The pressure is intense for him to be there for me and my family. He doesn't sleep.

Despairing, I tell him that if I don't leave, I will get violent. Casting around for any solution, feeling abandoned, I am so angry that I want to throw things and scream. I speak in a furiously even voice. I am ready to escape.

A doctor recommends recovering elsewhere and says, "You will deteriorate every additional night you spend here. You may get a hospital bug. When you leave, your nightmares will stop. This is not the place to heal."

On Day Six, I ace the readiness tests. Muscle training for twenty-seven years pays off—I climb two flights of stairs two days after coding. My surgeon pays a visit to reassure me . . . but it's my family that needs reassurance.

We come up with a solution: I will spend two weeks at a convalescent home. I swoon at the taste of real food. My nightmares stop. The pain ebbs and I take regular Tylenol. I am happy/angry/relieved. I need time to decompress from this assault on my body/nerves/senses.

For months I cry as much as I sleep—I grieve, letting go of fear of the hospital, of fear of dying before my kids are grown. I share with my cardiac rehab friends and Women@Heart sisters. There is a dying of habit, a quieting, then a sweet, slow rebirth.

My heart and soul are mending. I am a heart warrior; I fight for what I believe in. I focus on getting well. I love, sleep, write, and draw. I swim in warm waters. I hike and appreciate every breath I take. I marry my sweetheart and surprise my daughters with crazy ideas, drawings, and emotions.

Each morning I wake up slowly, savoring the shift from dreamtime to daytime. I breathe with awareness. I appreciate the small things in life. I call my mother every day and ask what's new, and she always says, "I'm alive!" I check if she's taken her pills, and sometimes she talks about the boy she kissed when she was young. This is precious to me.

I answer an important question: To be? Oh, yes. I embrace life.

Karen J. Watson, BA, BFA, has been a visual artist, a government communications manager, and a writer. She is currently synthesizing life-and-death experiences. Her side hustles include hospice volunteer, heart surgery survivor, parent, and caregiver. She is a fierce defender of all that is lively. Karen lives with her husband in Ottawa, Canada.

www.kjwatson.ca

BELIEVE YOUR WAY TO GREATNESS AND SUCCESS

Natasha E. Williams

It was early March 2020, before the announcement of the global pandemic in the United States. I was visiting my mother in Louisiana; however, this particular trip would be different than previous ones. One day my brother looked at me and said, "You look rich."

That comment took me by surprise because I wasn't expecting it, nor did I consider myself "rich" at all. I was dressed very casually and not wearing anything expensive.

"Why do you say that?" I asked.

"It's just the way you carry yourself," he replied.

I believe it is the self-confidence I have developed over the years that manifests on the outside. Being "rich" is subjective and different for everyone. For me, being rich means being able to live a life of ease, without financial worries or concerns, under my own terms. I am indeed living the life of my dreams. I am doing a job I love, I have traveled to sixty countries, I am healthy, and I am financially stable and building wealth.

But it hasn't always been that way.

You see, I grew up poor, below the poverty line in Louisiana in the Deep South. My earliest memory is circa 1977 when I was about eight years old. My grandmother worked all her life as a housekeeper, washwoman, and ironing lady for several wealthy families. On one particular day while accompanying my grandmother on an errand, we encountered one of the women she worked for. My grandmother greeted the lady and introduced me.

The lady smiled as she leaned over and asked, "Are you going to clean my house, too, when you grow up?" I looked at the lady dead in her eyes and said, "No, ma'am. I'm going to go to college. I'm going to be somebody one day!" Shocked, the lady gave my grandmother a stern look, rolled her eyes, and quickly walked away.

Looking back, I believe those words came from the depths of my soul. Even at that young age, I knew I wanted to do more than simply "get by" financially. I wanted to be more than a washwoman, and I knew that education was the key to break down the doors of poverty.

As I grew older, it became clear that education was not the only thing that was needed. Changing my mindset would play a larger role in my growth and development that would ultimately lead to the success I desired. What good is education if your life is still centered on a lack mentality and limiting beliefs?

I did not realize how poor I was until I went away to university. In the environment I grew up in, everyone basically lived the same way. However, although my family was poor, we always had food to eat, a place to live, and clothes on our backs. Although my family was not highly educated, they were hard workers. My great-grandmother even saved enough money to buy a home back in the day when it was difficult for colored people (as they were known in those days) to get financing. Through hard work and sacrifice, my grandparents were able to provide a carefree childhood for my brother and me, so we did not feel impoverished.

That realization motivated me to be the first person in my family to obtain a higher education and also change the way I responded to life. That realization was enforced when I ran across a book in a used bookstore called *The Power of Positive Thinking* by Norman Vincent Peale. From that point on, I believed in the totality of possibilities and in the belief that if I changed my thinking, my life would change for the better. The mind is a mighty mover, and I believe what we think about we bring about; therefore, from that day forward I began taking steps to make my dreams come true.

I was so excited about all the new possibilities I could create for my life and started to make five big, magnificent dreams for myself. I did not think about how they would manifest; I just wholeheartedly believed that they would. And I was right; each of them has come true. When I began telling others about my dreams, they either laughed in my face because they didn't see how I would be able to achieve them or simply told me I could never achieve what I set out to achieve. They could not see themselves achieving their dreams, so they projected that thought pattern on to me. I realized that small minds can't dream big dreams, and I stopped sharing my dreams with others.

So, whatever you set out to do, believe that you can do it if you set your heart on it, create goals, and take action. Don't let anyone tell you that you cannot achieve your dreams; do not let anybody rain on your parade, and certainly do not let anyone dull your sparkle.

Below are the steps I took. Following this simple roadmap will lead you on the path to living the life you've always dreamt of living.

1. Believe in yourself and in your talents and abilities.
2. Dream a remarkable dream and believe it will come true.
3. Set goals that push you toward your dream.
4. Establish a workable timeline for each step to keep you on track.
5. Be fearless, courageous, and steadfast. Be resilient! Never back down, no matter how tough things get or how impossible things may seem.
6. Be decisive and learn from your mistakes.
7. Be your own advocate. Make your own path where there seems to be none and don't look back.
8. Be prepared for opportunities that show up.
9. Never give up. Have the mindset that success is the only option and you will succeed.

I am living proof that dreams do come true. The secret to having everything starts with believing you already do!

Natasha E. Williams is an international speaker who has traveled to over sixty countries, an author who has sold projects to Hollywood, a coach serving on the development team for two Chicken Soup for the Soul® books, and the founder of the Think Rich Society, an online community for living a life of abundance.

www.thinkrichsociety.com

A Moment in Time That Changed My Life

Dr. Paulette Williams

My story is not about who I am today. It is about the woman who lay in the darkness at the bottom of a flight of stairs decades ago. It's about the woman who found her way out of darkness and transformed into the accomplished woman she is today.

The darkest period of my life started when I married a tall, dark, handsome military man. Shortly after our wedding, we moved to Germany to fulfill a military assignment and begin our lives together with the expectation that we would raise our children and grow old together.

One day my husband invited two of his buddies home for dinner. I was fussing over the guys and making sure they had enough to eat. Suddenly my husband grabbed me, pulled me out of the chair, slapped me across the face, opened the front door to the apartment, and threw me down a flight of stairs. As I lay at the bottom of the stairs, the two guys rushed down the stairs, stepped over me, and walked away.

I was thousands of miles from home with no one to confide in. I knew that if I called the commander, the consequence my husband would face would only make matters worse. I suddenly remembered my mother's warning: "If you make your bed hard, you have to lie in it."

For years I endured physical and verbal abuse. I reached my pivotal point when I heard my husband saying to our two-year-old son, "Look how dumb and stupid your mother is." I knew I did not want my son to grow up in an environment where it was okay to physically and mentally abuse women.

One night, after another physical fight, my husband stormed out the house. I went into the bathroom. I looked at the woman in the mirror, with red eyes and tears streaming down her cheeks, and I asked her the question,

"Do you want to live the rest of your life like this?" The woman replied between sobs, "NO!" This pivotal moment brought forth the strength within me to take action. I made a commitment to my son that I would find a way to remove both of us from this violent environment.

Three things helped me to rise from the darkness of domestic violence and take control of my life. The first was to **love myself.** It was challenging at first to love myself. I had been told so many times that I was worthless, that I could not do anything right, and that I would never amount to anything. Deep within, I knew that was not true. I started on a path to love myself. I took a mirror, looked into my eyes, and said to myself, "I am beautiful, I am smart, I am resilient, and I have a purpose for my life." As I practiced saying those words every day, I began to feel love for myself, and my purpose began to reveal itself. Over time I turned my purpose into my reality. There were roadblocks along the way; however, my sadness was replaced by light that became brighter and more brilliant with each passing day.

The second phase of my progress was **being in a state of gratitude.** I began to acknowledge the goodness I experienced moment to moment. It could be as simple as waking up each morning and giving thanks for the new day or softly saying "thank you" when I found a parking space in a full lot. At the end of each day, as I reflected on my blessings, my heart filled with joy. I learned to appreciate all the blessings, no matter how small, and pay them forward.

Finally, I discovered the power of **forgiveness.** I started by forgiving myself. I forgave my ex-husband. I learned to feel grateful for what my experience with him taught me. I learned to protect myself and my son, to make my own decisions, and to pursue my life's purpose.

Once I had a clear understanding of my purpose, I returned to school and earned my master's and doctorate degrees. I joined the military and served for twenty-three years as an Army nurse. I raised my son as a single parent. I am proud to say that he is a loving husband, the caring father of two, and has earned his master's degree in Family and Marriage Counseling.

You or someone you know has or will experience domestic violence. According to the Centers for Disease Control, one out of every six women and one out of every nine men will experience domestic violence in their lifetime. We must break through the darkness of shame and hopelessness associated with domestic violence and enter the light of courage, confidence, and dignity. It can be done. I am living proof.

I invite you to uncover your strength. Rediscover self-love. Begin the journey of discovering your purpose in life. Everyone has a unique path. Start your journey toward your chosen path. When obstacles cross your path, believe that you have the strength, wisdom, and power to see yourself through. When you are living your life's purpose, the darkness of shame and hopelessness will be replaced with joy—joy in knowing you have become the person you dreamed you could be.

I am Dr. Paulette Williams. I am not that woman at the bottom of the stairs feeling isolated, violated, and helpless. I am an elegant and educated woman who stayed the course and pushed through adversities. I discovered that with love of self, gratitude, and forgiveness, I could transform myself into the person I envisioned. I stand before you today as a beacon of light, knowing that you, too, can find your inner strength and transform into the person you desire to be.

Dr. Paulette Williams is a retired Army Nurse Lieutenant Colonel, retired nursing professor, and founder of Coach with Dr. Paulette. Dr. Williams blends her wisdom as a nurse with heartfelt coaching techniques. She empowers her clients to shift from contemplation to focused, inspired actions.

www.coachwithdrpaulette.com

THE RESILIENCE FACTOR

Kamini Wood

Resilience is defined as "the capacity to recover quickly from difficulties; toughness." Another way of looking at resilience is to think of the way a rubber band can be stretched very far but has the ability to rebound to its original shape, so long as it's not stretched beyond its capacity.

Being stretched too thin is something that I personally have been working on the last few years. As a people pleaser, one of the many things I tend to do is continually add to my plate, hour by hour, adding more and more. Then the feeling of needing to finish and clear all the things from my plate would take over my thoughts.

It's somewhat equivalent and reminiscent of when I was younger and told if I had put food on my plate, I needed to finish it. And I needed to avoid lolling around and finish as quickly as I could. Fast-forward to adulthood, I would view all I added to my life's plate and believe that it all needed to be accomplished and there was some type of unspoken race to the finish line.

As I've worked through my people-pleasing perfectionism, one theme kept reappearing: It was okay to "have leftovers" for later. It was okay not to get to everything on my plate. And it was equally okay to stop adding to my plate when it felt full already.

As a mother of five myself, I reflect a lot on what today's youth are growing through and how things have changed and evolved from when I was young. One thing I have noticed is that their plates seem even fuller that I recall mine ever being. And it seems as though they are expected to maintain a full plate while the world is spinning them around and twisting and turning at a fever pace.

Right now, as I am writing this, we are living through "unprecedented times"—a global pandemic has basically shut down whole nations at a time. Children have had to shift from going to a brick-and-mortar school to learning the same material virtually, socially separated from their peers and having their extracurriculars put on an indefinite hold.

In essence, by its mere presence, the pandemic has emptied the extracurricular activities from our kids' plates but added even more by way of needing to learn in a whole new way. Teens have a new added pressure of maintaining their GPAs while meandering through the trial-and-error of online learning, possibly figuring out how to prepare for and take AP exams. If they planned on playing a college sport, they are now faced with unknowns of how to get recruited if their sport is not allowed to compete—and the list goes on.

From my personal perspective, I can say that I have never had to call upon my own resilience more, and I've watched my kids tap into theirs.

Given the new circumstances and pressures of all the unknowns, the default way I would have typically shown up would have been to attempt to handle a full work schedule, completely handle all the house management, and take on all the online school management as well. In brutal honesty, that's what I tried to when the pandemic started, but very quickly I remembered that carrying a full plate and feeling like everything had to be done, and done perfectly, does not serve me well. In fact, it hinders me from facing adversity. I had to anchor into my new way of showing up, which was to admit that it's okay to admit when I'm feeling overwhelmed. It is also equally okay to ask for support and to realize I am not alone. These things actually raise the resiliency factor and help me face the adversity.

Likewise, I realized that I needed to empower my children to do the same. It is just as important for them to see that they can and should seek out assistance when they need it, and they should not try to do all the things and do them all perfectly.

In order to raise our resiliency and be able to meet adversity, we need to be able to ask for help. And even more—we need to be able to ask for help without self-judgment.

Brené Brown put it best when she said during a TEDxHouston talk, "When you cannot accept and ask for help without self-judgment, then when you offer other people help, you are always doing so with judgment. Always. Because you have attached judgment to asking for help."

Resiliency is not about never feeling stress or overwhelm. It is about how we face it and "snap" back from those feelings. During this pandemic, it has become very clear that we have to evaluate what we are focusing on. What we are thinking? What we are feeling? Are those things keeping us stuck? And what do we need?

Far too often we feel stuck when we ask ourselves, "*How* can I get through this? *How* do I make sense of the struggle or adversity I am facing?" Resiliency and the ability to see life's challenges as growth opportunities come with breaking down that *how* into honesty with oneself, openmindedness to what is possible, and a willingness to shift when necessary.

Building our resiliency requires a few mindset shifts. First, we need to give ourselves permission to choose what we are going to add to our plate, what we will drop, and how we will change course if needed. Second, we must allow for flexible thinking about situations, asking ourselves, "Is there another way to look at this?" Third, we need to be able to ask for support when we need it. Additionally, we have to be okay with feeling the uncomfortableness that rides alongside uncertainty. And finally, when we ask for help, we must do so without self-judgment, and likewise offer help without judging others. From there . . . resilience grows.

Kamini Wood, a mother of five, is an international bestselling author, and a certified life coach for teens and adults. Board certified through the AADP, as founder and CEO of Live Joy Your Way and the AuthenticMe® RiseUp program, she works with high achievers on letting go of stress, overwhelm, and anxiety.

www.itsauthenticme.com

BOOK CLUB CONVERSATION STARTERS

This book, *Voices of the 21st Century*, offers wisdom and inspiration to rise above circumstances and make a difference. To support you and your book club members, you may choose to use the following questions to start a discussion about sharing your powerful voice and making a bigger difference.

1. Resilient women have shared their stories of rising. What resilient woman has been an inspiration in your life and why?

2. Which of the stories brought you to tears? Laughter? Deep thought? What in particular moved you to each of these?

3. What does resilience mean to you? Has your definition changed since reading these stories?

4. What causes and messages are you most passionate about? What experiences in your life led to this passion?

5. What next steps are you inspired to take to make a difference? Would you like to do that in collaboration?

6. If you were to write a story, chapter, or book, what would you write about? What impact would you like it to have on others?

7. Given your passions and the ways you've been resilient, what organizations might you become involved with?

8. How will you further your leadership in your family, community, region, etc.?

What is your story?
If you'd like to share it within a collective like this book,
visit **VoicesOfThe21stCentury.com**
to find out how you and/or your group can participate.

VOICES OF THE 21ST CENTURY

Voices of the 21st Century is published annually by women from around the world who share their voice and message and offer insights, hope, wisdom, and inspiration.

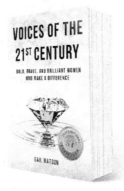

Women Who Influence, Inspire, and Make a Difference

Bold, Brave, and Brilliant Women Who Make a Difference

available at

amazon

Powerful, Passionate Women Who Make a Difference

See the authors and their bios listed at
voicesofthe21stcenturybook.com

Are You a Global Business Connector?

Women Speakers Association is seeking ten women to license and represent their city as a WSA GLOBAL BUSINESS CONNECTOR. This program is designed for you to own your own speaking platform, leverage the global brand, elevate your presence and reach, and amplify your marketing to increase your bottom line.

As the #1 platform for getting your message heard, WSA provides a Global Success System for members to clarify, market, and monetize their message. As a Global Business Connector, you'll be trained, licensed, and supported to hold live events in your city, build your own community, and provide WSA members with access to the tools, resources, and training for growing their business.

This business opportunity has a potential six-figure return on investment! And takes what you're already doing, accelerates, and amplifies your results. You are investing in a complete and proven plug-and-play marketing system.

We Want You!

This is perfect for you if you already have an established business or network and you are looking for ways to expand your reach and revenue potential.

 To learn more visit: wsalive.com

CPSIA information can be obtained
at www.ICGtesting.com
Printed in the USA
LVHW081353210321
682028LV00046B/1685